The Practical DBT Guide for Adult Mental Health

A Proven Approach to Stop Overthinking, Boost Self-Esteem, and Improve Social Skills with Emotional Intelligence and Positive Psychology

Eve Mason

SPECIAL BONUS!!
Want this book for FREE?

Get **FREE** and unlimited access to
it and all of my new books by joining the
Fan Base

Scan w/ your
camera to join!

Table of Contents

Introduction

Mental health is an important issue that affects millions of adults around the world. Mental health issues, such as depression, anxiety, and bipolar disorder, can impact an individual's day-to-day life, relationships, and productivity. Unfortunately, these mental health issues can often go unnoticed, especially in adults. Without proper diagnosis and treatment, mental health problems can worsen over time, leading to increased stress and emotional distress and making it more difficult for the individual to maintain their physical and emotional well-being. Imagine having brain cancer and walking around without knowing that the disease is slowly killing you. Cancer will inevitably trigger the deterioration of your body, and your body will stay that way over time if you don't get it treated. Mental health problems act the exact same way, and they should be given as much care and attention as traditional illnesses and diseases.

In addition to mental health issues that can lead to emotional distress, there are various lifestyle-related problems that may also contribute to mental health problems in adults. Many adults find it difficult to balance their work lives and personal lives, leading to feelings of loneliness or isolation. Reliance on drugs or alcohol as a coping mechanism is another common problem, which only helps to worsen an existing mental health issue. It is essential that adults are aware of the signs of mental health issues and understand the importance of seeking appropriate treatment. More than just being aware, it's essential that adults know how to address their mental health problems as early as possible. However, the problem persists that not many adults know how to address these problems or even where to begin. This is exactly where this book comes in.

Dialectical behavioral therapy (DBT) is a type of therapy that is used to help people better manage their emotions and behaviors. It combines cognitive behavioral therapy techniques with mindfulness skills. This form of therapy focuses on accepting one's thoughts and attitudes and changing them for the better. It helps people learn how to identify, accept, and regulate their emotions; increase their self-awareness; and develop better interpersonal skills. Ultimately, DBT can help individuals gain insight, learn healthier behaviors, and build better relationships. Throughout this book, we will be using principles of DBT to help shed further insight into how you can manage your mental health for the better in a simple and sustainable fashion.

The primary benefit of DBT is that it provides you with the skills to help manage your emotions, cope with life's difficulties, and interact more effectively with others. It's focused on helping you learn mindful awareness, emotion regulation, distress tolerance, and interpersonal effectiveness. Mindfulness in DBT focuses on helping you be more aware of the present moment. This can help you become less reactive and instead slow down to assess how you're feeling and what might be the most appropriate response. Emotion regulation helps you identify and label your emotions, as well as learn how to manage yourself in difficult emotional situations. You'll be taught how to prevent negative emotions and healthily process high degrees of stress. Distress tolerance provides you with a range of strategies to help you accept and manage intense emotions in a more constructive way. It helps you recognize that sometimes it's not possible to change a situation right away, so it's important to be aware of your perceptions around these events to better understand yourself. Interpersonal effectiveness focuses on teaching you strategies to help you communicate your needs and feelings assertively. You'll practice how to ask for what you want, say no to unwanted requests, and how to effectively negotiate with others.

To illustrate the effectiveness of DBT, let's talk about the story of Nazie. Nazie had been struggling with her mental health since she was a teenager; she felt disconnected from the world and frustrated by her inability to cope with the daily struggles of life. She had tried many treatments over the years; however, nothing had ever made a lasting difference. That all changed when she started seeing her therapist, who encouraged her to try DBT. Nazie was hesitant at first but soon realized the value in using the therapy skills.

Through weekly sessions with her therapist, Nazie started to manage her stress more effectively, cope with her emotions with more clarity, and build a support system of family and friends to help her navigate difficult times. She began to take greater pleasure in activities that she used to find mundane and reconnect with the joy of living. Gradually, Nazie was able to look at complicated situations from multiple perspectives and view her difficulties through a more positive lens. She was able to have meaningful conversations with those around her and no longer felt so isolated and lonely.

Nazie is now thriving in her life and is thankful for the changes DBT allowed her to make. She looks forward to her weekly sessions with her therapist and applies the skills she learned to her everyday life. She is living a more fulfilling and meaningful life thanks to DBT.

In all honesty, *Nazie* is a hypothetical character. However, just because she's fictional doesn't mean that her story isn't based on reality. There are so many real people who have stories exactly like Nazie's who have managed to find fulfillment in life as a result of DBT. It's important to see yourself in Nazie's narrative as well. You have the ability to have a dramatic and fulfilling narrative similar to the hypothetical one we just laid out. All of that starts with understanding the problem that you're facing and what you need to do to methodically address it. This book will help open your eyes to the wonders of DBT and how you can apply this in your everyday life. The road to better mental health starts here.

Chapter 1:

The Mental Health Concept

We all have mental health, just like we have physical health. Many of us have some knowledge of common mental health disorders and illnesses, but there is much more we can understand about the complexity of this area of health and well-being. In this chapter, we'll explore the different concepts and theories that can help us understand mental health, the various causes and types of mental illnesses, and why it is so important for us to gain a better understanding of these matters. With this in-depth look at mental health, we can gain a greater appreciation of its importance and how it affects our lives and the lives of those around us.

Mental health is an issue that is not discussed enough in today's society, and this is a problem that has to change. Mental health is an integral part of our lives, and it is something that needs to be taken seriously and addressed in order for people to be able to live their lives in a healthy and productive way.

Unfortunately, the stigma surrounding mental health makes it difficult for people to talk about it openly and honestly. Mental health conditions can be seen as signs of weakness or of being "crazy," making it hard for people to be honest about their feelings and experiences. This is especially true for men, who are often taught from a young age to just "suck it up" and be strong, no matter what.

The lack of dialogue surrounding mental health also makes it hard for people to reach out in times of need. Mental health is often seen as something that shouldn't be discussed, which can make it difficult for people to find the help and resources that they need.

Ultimately, the conversation surrounding mental health needs to change. We need to create an environment where it is okay to talk openly about mental health and where people can seek the help that they need without judgment. This can only be achieved by having open and honest conversations about mental health in order to educate the public and reduce the stigma. We need to make sure that no one ever feels ashamed or embarrassed to talk about mental health and that everyone is made aware that mental health issues are not uncommon and are treatable and manageable.

It is absolutely okay and necessary to acknowledge if you are not doing well mentally. It is important to be aware of your mental health, and it is nothing to be ashamed of. It's easy to brush off signs of mental distress, but if you recognize how you're feeling and take the necessary steps to address it, you can lead a happier and healthier life.

It's important to talk to someone about your mental health, whether that is a friend, a family member, or even a mental health professional. Seeking help is an indicator of strength and courage rather than weakness. Additionally, you can try to address your mental health needs yourself by participating in activities that make you feel relaxed, such as yoga, meditation, or journaling as a way to work through your thoughts and feelings.

No matter how you choose to tackle your mental health concerns, it is important to know that it is okay to acknowledge when you are not doing well mentally. Taking care of yourself is the first and most crucial step in the process, and you should never feel ashamed or embarrassed about seeking help for your mental health.

Why Mental Health Is Crucial to One's Overall Health

Mental health is an essential part of overall health and well-being. It affects how we think, feel, and act in our daily lives. Mental health is closely linked to physical health, as poor mental health can lead to

includes five fundamental states of mental health: resilience, vulnerability, well-being, illness, and recovery.

Resilience

The concept of resilience refers to a person's capacity to successfully deal with difficult or challenging life experiences. It is closely linked to the ability to cope with stress, adversity, and trauma while maintaining positive mental health and functioning. Resilience is a quality that helps individuals to effectively navigate stressful situations and to recover quickly from setbacks. This capacity is seen as central to maintaining overall well-being and mental health.

At its core, building resilience involves cultivating the capacity to effectively manage and regulate emotional responses, identifying and implementing effective coping strategies, and understanding one's emotional and psychological functioning. Furthermore, it involves developing effective communication and problem solving abilities; connecting with supportive networks of family, friends, and professionals; building meaningful relationships; and engaging in self-care and meaningful activities. These skills and abilities can help an individual to effectively manage difficult life experiences and reduce their risk of developing mental health difficulties.

Vulnerability

Vulnerability has to do with an individual's susceptibility to physical, psychological, and emotional distress that can occur as a result of stressors associated with their environment and/or their own mental health. It is based on the idea that certain factors—such as genetics, neurobiology, environment—and social context can all affect an individual's vulnerability.

CSM identifies three primary states of vulnerability, which are termed "primary vulnerability," "modifiable vulnerability," and "protective vulnerability." Primary vulnerability is the baseline state of an individual's susceptibility to mental health issues. It is largely determined by biology, genetics, or environment. Modifiable vulnerability is the state of an individual's susceptibility to mental health issues that are determined by their present circumstances such as stress exposure and lifestyle changes. Protective vulnerability is the state of an individual's susceptibility to mental health issues that are determined by assets that can help protect an individual from the effects of stressors. These assets can include access to social support, positive coping strategies, and healthy physical and mental health behaviors.

By understanding the three different states of vulnerability, it is possible to develop strategies and interventions tailored to an individual's current state of vulnerability. This allows for more effective, individualized mental health treatments that can be better tailored to an individual's particular needs.

Well-Being

Well-being is a state of mental health that is characterized by both subjective and objective components. Subjectively, it is an individual's assessment of their life satisfaction and sense of positive emotions such as contentment, hope, and joy. Objectively, it is the quality of physical and mental health, functional capacity, life circumstances, and quality of relationships with family, friends, and community.

Physical health refers to the overall condition of the body and how able it is to be in shape, fight disease, and heal itself. Mental health involves psychological functioning, thought processes, and emotions, and it is achieved when mental balance is maintained. Social health is derived from the quality of relationships in our lives, the kinds of activities we take part in, and the satisfaction we gain from our life circumstances.

The goal of achieving well-being is to create a positive balance between all of these components. It involves developing positive skills and attitudes in each area while paying attention to the needs of the body, mind, and social life. With improved physical health, mental health, and stronger relationships, individuals can live life to its fullest potential while still feeling content. They can experience sensations of joy, hope, self-confidence, and a sense of purpose as they move through life. This state of well-being is not a destination but an ongoing journey, and it is necessary for an individual to reach their fullest potential.

Illness

CSM is a theoretical framework that defines mental health as the complete state of well-being, which involves the integration of psychological, emotional, and behavioral functioning. When considering illness, the model suggests that mental health problems arise when there is a disruption or imbalance in one or more of these areas.

Psychological functioning refers to an individual's cognitive processes, including perception, memory, reasoning, problem-solving, decision-making, and personality traits. When an individual experiences mental health problems, they may struggle with these cognitive processes. For example, they may experience difficulty concentrating or have distorted thinking patterns. This can impact their overall mental health and contribute to the development of mental illnesses such as depression or anxiety disorders.

Emotional functioning refers to an individual's ability to experience, express, and regulate their emotions. Mental health problems can disrupt emotional functioning, leading to intense and prolonged emotional states. For example, an individual with depression may experience a pervasive feeling of sadness, while an individual with bipolar disorder may experience extreme mood swings.

Behavioral functioning refers to an individual's observable actions and responses to the environment. Mental health problems can impact behavioral functioning, leading to maladaptive behaviors such as social withdrawal, substance abuse, or self-harm. For example, an individual with an eating disorder may engage in compulsive behaviors such as binge eating or purging.

Recovery

Finally, recovery emphasizes the role of resilience, hope, and personal strength in managing and overcoming mental health issues. It views mental health as a fluid and dynamic construct that involves ongoing adaptive processes. Recovery is the process of learning to cope with, adjust to, and manage mental health challenges, and it involves a combination of self-management strategies, utilization of support networks, and mental health treatments. Recovery focuses on living life to the fullest potential despite the realities of mental health issues. It is a holistic approach that recognizes the needs of the mind, body, and spirit and involves experimentation and collaboration to find the best ways to promote successful outcomes. It recognizes that an individual may experience both good days and bad days and works to support positive experiences regardless of circumstance. Furthermore, recovery emphasizes the notion that individuals can take control of their mental health and actively participate in their own recovery journey.

CSM provides a comprehensive understanding of mental health and proposes an integrative approach to promoting healthy functioning, reducing vulnerability, and supporting recovery. This model incorporates both individual and contextual factors and emphasizes the need to create supportive and protective environments to promote mental health.

Other Mental Health Theories and Models

Aside from CSM, there are also other reputable mental health theories and models that are widely recognized and accepted within the community, including cognitive behavioral therapy (CBT), psychodynamic theory and model, and the biopsychosocial model.

Cognitive Behavioral Therapy (CBT)

Cognitive behavioral therapy is a type of psychotherapy based on the idea that our thoughts, feelings, and behaviors are connected. This means that by understanding and changing our thoughts and beliefs, we can also change our emotions and behavior. CBT has been found to be effective in helping people manage mental health issues, including depression, anxiety, and post-traumatic stress disorder, among many others.

An example of CBT might involve a therapist working with a person who is struggling with anxiety. The therapist works with the individual in order to identify the thoughts and beliefs that fuel their anxious feelings. The person might feel like they're not good enough or that they're not deserving of certain things. The therapist then helps them challenge and reframe these beliefs and thought patterns, allowing them to find more productive ways of thinking about their situation. For instance, rather than focusing on their weaknesses, the individual might start to think, "I can handle this. I just need to take one step at a time." Once the person has adopted a more positive mindset and found ways of expressing and processing their feelings, they are better able to manage their anxiety.

CBT is a structured form of psychotherapy that encourages people to become active participants in the process of reducing their distress. Its focus on self-reflection, improving problem-solving skills, and setting realistic goals has been proven to help people learn to manage their mental health and make lasting changes in their lives.

Psychodynamic Theory

Psychodynamic theory originated in the work of Sigmund Freud, a neurologist and influential psychoanalyst. Freud proposed that the human psyche is made up of three components: the id, the ego, and the superego. The id is located in the unconscious and is responsible for manifesting our most basic desires. The ego is the conscious part of the psyche and helps us to deal with reality and negotiate the tension between the desires of the id and the values of the superego. The superego is the part of the psyche that represents societal morals and values, and it is responsible for constraining the desires of the id.

This psychological theory focuses on how unconscious processes and hidden motives, often related to development in childhood, drive behavior and impact mental health. It is based on the premise that the conscious and the unconscious are intertwined and that events that occur in our present and past impact our behavior and how we think and interact with others. This theory implies that much of our behavior is influenced by unconscious forces and processes; for example, an individual may act differently at work or in public than they do in private or with family. This can be attributed to the fact that different people hold different values in different places and roles and may be subconsciously worried that expressing certain behavior or desires may be socially unacceptable. Therefore, they repress these feelings in the presence of certain people or in a certain context.

Biopsychosocial Model

The biopsychosocial model is a widely accepted model that looks at the interaction among biological, psychological, and social factors which influence a person's health and well-being. It was first developed by Dr. George Engel in 1977, who argued that mental health and emotional well-being should be studied in light of both internal and external influences. This model takes into account the unique experiences of an individual and the various aspects of their life. It is not only used in psychology but also plays a role in understanding a wide range of physical, mental, and social health issues.

This model is made up of three main components: biological, psychological, and social. The biological component focuses on the relationship between our physical health and physiological states. This includes genetics, nutrition, hormones, and other physiological factors that may affect our psychological and social states. The psychological component looks at how our thoughts, feelings, and behaviors may influence our biological components. This incorporates factors like anxiety and depression, self-esteem, and cognitive tendencies. Finally, the social element explores interactions with family, friends, cultural beliefs, and education and how these things influence one's disposition.

For example, say a person was feeling depressed. There could be multiple sources of evidence for this within the biopsychosocial model. First, there could be a biological component, such as a nutritional deficiency or an imbalance in hormones. On the psychological level, the individual may have a negative outlook on life and face difficulties with their self-esteem. Last, on the social level, the individual may not have much close contact or social support. All the different components must be taken into consideration in order to fully understand the person's depression and devise a treatment plan.

The Concepts of Mental Health

Mental health is the combination of emotional and social well-being, and it can be described as a state of balanced and resilient functioning. Mental health is essential for the overall well-being and functioning of an individual and encompasses a person's abilities to manage and cope with life's challenges on an emotional, cognitive, and behavioral level. It also includes an individual's ability to participate in and enjoy relationships and other positive aspects of life.

Contrary to what many people may believe, mental health is more than just the presence or absence of a mental health condition (such as depression or anxiety disorder). It involves having self-awareness and emotional regulation, the ability to thrive in relationships, and the ability to self-actualize and achieve personal goals. Mental health is a dynamic, changing state, and what is considered healthy for one person may be unhelpful for another.

For the most part, mental health is often described in terms of four broad domains: emotional, social, cognitive, and behavioral.

Emotional Well-Being

Emotional well-being is a state of psychological and physiological functioning associated with the absence of any form of distress, disease, or dysfunction in an individual. This state of psychological and physiological health allows individuals to experience positive emotions, such as joy, contentment, and enthusiasm. More specifically, emotional well-being is an individual's ability to respond in a balanced and appropriate manner to challenges, shocks, and stressors in life while maintaining the capacity to enjoy life and feel content. Mental health is closely related to emotional well-being and is largely affected by it. When an individual's emotional well-being is low, it can have detrimental effects on their mental health.

Social Well-Being

Social well-being is a measure of how people feel connected to their community and how they experience social inclusion. It can be affected by a range of factors, including but not limited to, relationships with family and friends, economic hardships, and social influence. The importance of social well-being in mental health has been recognized by researchers and clinicians alike due to its potential to aid in resiliency and reduce the need for interventions and treatments. Social connections provide individuals with emotional, social, and financial support, which can help them with coping when faced with difficult situations. Additionally, research has found that activities such as volunteering, physical and creative activities, sports, and socializing have an important impact on mental and emotional well-being (Thoreson, 2021).

Cognitive Well-Being

Cognitive well-being is a concept that is gaining momentum in the mental health field as it relates to overall mental well-being and functioning. This domain refers to the degree of cognitive functioning, including cognitive abilities, resources, and abilities, to be used in day-to-day life. It focuses on an individual's capacity to cope with stress every day while being able to adapt and respond to changing circumstances. Cognitive well-being can also refer to the ability to form and maintain meaningful relationships, to maintain a capacity for creativity, to self-reflect, and to manage one's emotions effectively.

Behavioral Well-Being

Behavioral well-being suggests that stress, health-risk behaviors, and illness can be reduced and even prevented through lifestyle changes and healthy behaviors, such as eating a balanced diet, exercising regularly, and participating in social activities. It also suggests that individuals should be educated regarding the importance of taking care of their physical, mental, and emotional health. On top of that, individuals should explore the variety of holistic approaches to health and well-being available to them, such as yoga and meditation, as well as evidence-based medical interventions if needed. This domain is ultimately based on the notion that physical and mental well-being can be promoted by emphasizing positive health behaviors.

The Barriers to Mental Health Care

While mental health is a serious issue that people need to acknowledge and come to terms with, there are certain barriers that prevent individuals from getting the kind of care that they truly need. The stigma surrounding mental health is one of the greatest barriers to people accessing essential care. This occurs when people who have or have had mental health issues are viewed or labeled negatively or when their condition or treatment is looked down upon by society. Stigma can be based on ignorance, prejudice, or fear and often leads to people being ashamed of their condition or ashamed to seek help.

Stigmas can manifest in a variety of ways including blatant insults and discrimination, people avoiding contact with those affected, and the negative connotations surrounding words used to describe mental health issues and the people who suffer from them. Furthermore, many people feel uncomfortable discussing mental health, which leads to reduced dialogue on the matter and a perpetuation of the stigma. This can be worsened by the wider culture and the media, which often presents mental health in a sensational manner or treats it as less of a serious medical condition than physical health.

The effect of this stigma is an apparent reticence to address mental health issues and seek help among those affected, with studies showing that only around 47% of people with mental health issues seek help (National Institute of Mental Health, 2022). An unwillingness to seek help stems from fear of discrimination in their social and professional lives, worries about being labeled as "mentally ill," and the belief that seeking help could somehow affect their job prospects or worsen their mental health.

Overall, it is clear that stigma surrounding mental health is a major barrier to people seeking help and accessing the care they need. In order to reduce the stigma, there needs to be more open dialogue about mental health to provide accurate information and dismantle negative preconceptions. Furthermore, it's essential that policy interventions are set up to help protect those seeking help from discrimination and marginalization and to increase awareness of the support available for people with mental health issues.

Aside from the stigma associated with mental health care, a lot of people with mental health issues just don't know where and how to seek proper care. Mental health issues can be difficult to identify, especially because many people with mental health issues are unaware of the signs and symptoms, and they don't know where or how to seek help. According to the National Institute of Mental Health (2022), one out of every five American adults are battling some form of mental illness. However, only 46.2% of these adults received mental health services. This lack of care is likely attributed to the fact that so many individuals are unaware of, or overwhelmed by, their options for seeking help.

The situation is made worse by the fact that mental health resources may be limited in certain communities and hard to access. For example, those without insurance or without sufficient funds to pay for private or out-of-pocket services may have a difficult time finding treatment. Additionally, many of the publicly-available mental health services are provided through hospitals and clinics where the duration of care might be limited. Thus, individuals may not always be able to get long-term help or even find care that is specifically tailored to their needs.

To put it simply, there are numerous barriers that can prevent individuals from seeking help for mental health issues, including a lack of knowledge about available mental health services, fear of stigma or judgment, and the cost associated with seeking treatment. By recognizing and addressing these challenges, more individuals can gain access to the care that is necessary for managing mental health issues.

Mental Health Illnesses and Their Causes

Mental health disorders are some of the most complex and difficult-to-understand medical conditions. They can have varied root causes, from biological to environmental, making them even harder to diagnose and treat effectively. This section of the book serves to provide a comprehensive overview of the wide range of mental health disorders, including descriptions of each illness and their likely causes.

Depression

Depression is a mental disorder characterized by persistently low mood and a loss of interest in activities that can affect a person's thoughts, behaviors, feelings, and sense of well-being. It commonly affects people's ability to work, study, or fulfill everyday roles or responsibilities. This condition is known to cause a persistent feeling of sadness and loss of interest. It can significantly impair an individual's emotional, cognitive, and physical functioning and lead to a range of emotional and physical problems.

The exact cause of depression is unknown, although it is believed to involve a combination of genetic, biological, environmental, and psychological factors. It is thought to be caused by an imbalance of certain chemicals in the brain, known as neurotransmitters, which are responsible for regulating mood. Stressful life events, such as the loss of a loved one, divorce, or loss of a job, can also trigger depression, as can long-term difficulties, such as severe financial stress or chronic illness. People with depression may also have a history of medical illnesses, such as heart disease or diabetes, and these illnesses may influence the individual's risk for depression.

Anxiety Disorder

Anxiety disorder is a mental health condition characterized by intense and excessive fear and worry, physical symptoms, and related behavioral changes. It is one of the most common mental health disorders and affects millions of people worldwide. The symptoms of this disorder often lead to significant distress, hampering work and social functioning; in extreme cases, it can require professional intervention.

Like depression, the exact causes of anxiety disorder remain unclear, but several possible factors have been identified. These may include genetic and hereditary influences, medical conditions, changes in brain chemistry, physical and sexual abuse, trauma, and difficult life experiences. Certain environmental factors, such as excessive use of stimulants and drug or alcohol abuse, also may increase the risk of developing an anxiety disorder. It is important to note that anxiety is a normal response to stressful or dangerous situations, but when the worry and fear become overwhelming and interfere with daily functioning, it becomes a disorder.

Bipolar Disorder

Bipolar disorder is a mental health condition that is marked by extreme shifts in mood, energy, activity levels, and the ability to carry out day-to-day tasks. Typically, people with bipolar disorder experience periods of high energy and activity (called manic or hypomanic episodes) interspersed with periods of low energy and activity (called depressive episodes). People who have bipolar disorder may also experience periods of normal mood and activity levels in between episodes.

Consistent with depression and anxiety disorder, bipolar disorder doesn't have a known exact cause. However, research points to a combination of biological, psychological, and environmental factors. Genetics can play a role, as people with a family history of bipolar disorder are more likely to develop the condition. Additionally, differences in brain structure, chemistry, and function, especially in regions connecting mood, thoughts, sleep, and behaviors, may predispose some people to develop bipolar disorder. Furthermore, stressful life events, such as the death of a loved one or a traumatic event, can trigger the onset or relapse of symptoms.

Schizophrenia

Schizophrenia is a chronic, severe, and disabling mental disorder that affects how a person thinks, feels, and behaves, according to the American Psychological Association (APA, 2022). People with schizophrenia may hear voices other people don't hear, speak in unusual ways, or have false beliefs. It is a highly complex mental disorder, and its precise causes are still largely unknown.

The APA states that schizophrenia is likely caused by a combination of genetic, psychological, and environmental factors (American Psychological Association, 2021). People with a family history of the disorder are more likely to develop it, which suggests a genetic link. People who have experienced childhood trauma, physical or sexual abuse, or neglect may also be at a greater risk for developing the disorder.

Abnormal functioning of certain neurotransmitters (chemical messengers in the brain) may also be involved in the development of schizophrenia. For example, low levels of dopamine, a neurotransmitter involved in regulating motivation and pleasure, have been linked to schizophrenia. Research also suggests that environmental factors, such as high levels of stress, may play a role in the development of schizophrenia.

Post-Traumatic Stress Disorder

Post-traumatic stress disorder (PTSD) is a mental health disorder triggered by a traumatic event, such as experiencing trauma or witnessing a traumatic event. It can cause a wide range of symptoms, including intrusive memories, flashbacks, nightmares, insomnia, emotional numbness, hypervigilance, increased startle response, social withdrawal, rage, and a decreased ability to trust or form relationships. Because PTSD is a speculation disorder, it cannot be diagnosed based on a single symptom. The condition is only diagnosed when a person displays symptoms in a cluster and has experienced a traumatic event.

The causes of PTSD are multifaceted and involve certain predisposing risk factors and the individual's cognitive, emotional, and physiological response to their exposure to the traumatic event. Research has fallen into three main categories of risk factors: biological, psychological, and environmental. Biological risk factors that contribute to the development of PTSD include genetics, gender, age, temperament, sociodemographic factors, pre-existing mental health issues, and physical health. Psychological factors include higher levels of stress related to the trauma, perceived control over the experience, and difficulty regulating emotions. Environmental factors include the type, duration, and magnitude of the trauma; social support; and availability of mental health care.

Chapter 2:

EQ vs IQ

In this chapter, we will explore the differences between emotional quotient (EQ), also known as emotional intelligence, and intelligence quotient (IQ) and examine how EQ can affect your mental health and interpersonal relationships.

For the most part, people often value the development of their IQ much more than they do the development of their EQ. People see IQ as a measure of how *smart* they are, but they often overlook the importance of EQ as the ability to understand and manage emotions.

This can be a problem because having a high EQ is essential for success in life. People with a high EQ often demonstrate greater self-awareness, better interpersonal skills, and better problem-solving abilities. When you develop your EQ, you are also better able to identify, manage, and express your emotions in a healthy way, rather than ignoring them or being overwhelmed by them. This makes you better able to create and maintain meaningful relationships in your personal and professional lives.

In other words, having a high EQ makes it easier for someone to navigate their emotions in a constructive way, so they can handle difficult situations more effectively and develop more meaningful relationships. This can be a crucial tool for success in life; yet a lot of people don't recognize the value of it and instead prioritize developing their IQ.

In this chapter, we will talk all about what emotional intelligence is and the many ways that it can be manifested in real life. Aside from that, we will dive deeper into the theoretical models of emotional intelligence in order to give us a better idea of how it works and what we can do with it. Of course, we will also discuss the differences between IQ and EQ and the nuances of each. Just because this chapter is promoting the development of your EQ doesn't mean that IQ isn't important. Rather, the point of this chapter is to emphasize the fact that both traits go hand in hand with one another. As you develop one, you need to develop the other in order to lead a holistic and well-rounded life.

What Is Emotional Intelligence?

Emotional intelligence (EI), also known as emotional quotient, is the ability to recognize, understand, and manage emotions. It is an important part of your social and emotional development. EI involves a set of specific competencies, such as understanding different emotional expressions and feelings, adapting to different social and interpersonal situations, and recognizing and responding to the emotional needs of others.

At its core, emotional intelligence is about being able to identify, use, understand, and manage emotions, both in ourselves and in others. This involves recognizing and understanding emotions as they are expressed in others, as well as recognizing and understanding our own emotional states and their effects. It also involves us being able to use emotional information to lead, relate to, and influence our lives and the lives of others.

For example, being able to recognize when someone is upset and responding in a kind and empathetic way is putting your emotional intelligence to work. Being able to effectively communicate with others and form strong relationships also requires strong emotional intelligence. In all different kinds of situations throughout daily life, emotional intelligence must be used to navigate emotional and interpersonal dynamics. Being able to recognize emotions in oneself and others, understand the nuances of different emotional expressions, and respond with appropriate actions will enable positive relationships and successful living.

The Three Models of Emotional Intelligence

As you've already learned, EI is a multi-dimensional construct consisting of cognitive processes and abilities related to recognizing, understanding, and managing emotions. It is the ability to process, analyze, and utilize emotions so that you can be aware of your own emotions, as well as be able to control and respond to the emotions of those around you in order to be more socially skilled. Over the years, several different models of EI have been proposed in order to better understand how this construct works.

The Ability Model

The first model of emotional intelligence is the ability model. This is the oldest and most widely accepted model of EI, which is based on the idea that EI is a cognitive ability that people can improve through training and experiences. This model defines EI as a set of abilities, which include the recognition of emotions in oneself, the recognition of emotions in others, and the management of one's own and others' emotions. This model has been used to measure EI in research and in clinical applications.

The Trait Model

The second model is the trait model. This model serves as an alternative to the ability model. This model is based on the idea that EI is a personality trait, or a set of characteristics, that an individual possesses to a certain degree and that is relatively stable over time and across contexts. This model defines EI in terms of dispositional qualities related to understanding and managing emotions, such as interpersonal skills and empathy.

The Mixed Model

The third model is the mixed model. This model acts as a combination of the ability and trait models. This model suggests that EI is both a skill set that can be learned and improved as well as a personality trait that is relatively stable and consistent over time. This model includes both cognitive awareness and evaluation of emotions. Cognitive awareness is a mental ability in which individuals are able to recognize their own thought patterns and behaviors and make adjustments to them if necessary. Evaluation of emotions is the process of analyzing and assessing the feelings someone is experiencing in order to gain a better understanding of the situation or person.

Emotional Intelligence vs Intelligence Quotient

Earlier, we briefly touched on the idea that people mostly value working on their IQ as opposed to their EQ, which is also popularly known as emotional intelligence. All sorts of different academic tests are conducted in formal education in order to measure your IQ during your development as a student. For the most part, schools have a tendency to favor IQ tests and exams as opposed to their EQ counterparts. As a result, few kids put a premium on the development of their EQ as they get older. But what do these two traits really mean, and how do they individually impact your development as a human being overall?

Emotional intelligence and intelligence quotient are two different types of intelligence. Emotional intelligence is the ability to recognize, understand, and manage emotions in ourselves and in others. It is composed of the ability to be aware of and to express emotions, the ability to understand emotions and to have empathy for the emotions of others, and the ability to regulate our own emotions and those of others. On the other hand, IQ is a measure of a person's cognitive intelligence. It is measured by a standardized test that assesses a person's problem-solving, reasoning, and memorization skills to measure logical and abstract thinking.

Although it may appear that EI and IQ measure the same thing, the two concepts differ in that EI measures a person's ability to interpret, use, understand, and manage emotions, and IQ measures the person's raw cognitive ability. EI measures the degree to which we use our emotions and feelings in an appropriate manner to manage both ourselves and those with whom we interact, while IQ measures the ability to perform certain intellectual tasks that require logical thinking and analytical prowess. These two forms of intelligence may be related. For instance, it has been found that individuals with higher IQs tend to have higher levels of emotional intelligence (Heingartner, 2020). However, having a high level of one does not guarantee the presence of the other.

To put these two traits into perspective, imagine that you're a person who works in customer service. In order to be successful, you need to have a good EI in order to manage difficult conversations with customers, remain professional and courteous, and resolve conflicts. But having a high EI is not enough; you also need a high IQ in order to understand complex requests and problems that customers may have and be able to quickly think of a solution.

In this case, having both a high EI and IQ can help you to excel in the customer service field. Although you need to be able to recognize the emotions of your customers, you also need to be intelligent enough to be able to solve the problems your customers present.

What Emotional Intelligence Means for Your Mental Health

Emotional intelligence is a trait that is especially important in the context of mental health, as it can help people to better assess, comprehend, and manage their stress and emotions, which leads to improved outcomes such as better problem-solving, decision-making, and communication.

In the context of mental health, this trait is divided into different categories: self-awareness, self-regulation, motivation, social awareness, relationship management, social skills, and empathy. Self-awareness involves the ability to recognize and understand your own emotions and how they can influence your behavior. Self-regulation is the ability to control and manage emotions and impulses, while maintaining the ability to make reasoned decisions. When you can respond in a healthy way to negative and positive emotions, you hold yourself accountable and take responsibility for your actions. You also become better able to process your feelings without letting them control you. Motivation refers to the capacity to recognize and pursue goals even when faced with obstacles.

Social awareness is the understanding and sensitivity toward the ideas, needs, and perspectives of other people. Relationship management is the ability to build, maintain, and develop relationships with others. You know how to develop and maintain good relationships, communicate clearly, inspire and influence others, work well in a team, and manage conflict. Social skills are the ability to interact effectively with others and build meaningful relationships. Strong emotional intelligence allows you to have healthy relationships with others. Connection is a key to thriving in addiction recovery. Finally, empathy is the capacity to understand and recognize the emotions of other people. You can understand the emotions, needs, and concerns of other people, pick up on emotional cues, feel comfortable socially, and recognize the power dynamics in a group or organization.

By developing these core EI skills, you can better manage difficult emotions and thoughts, have more control over your behavior and decisions, and enhance your interpersonal connections. Mental health can also be improved by recognizing and accepting emotions as they arise instead of trying to suppress them. Finally, EI can also promote a greater sense of psychological well-being, as it allows individuals to understand themselves better, which leads to less negative self-judgment and an improved sense of personal agency.

As humans, we possess varying degrees of ability to understand our own emotions and the emotions of others. With this in mind, developing your emotional intelligence can be beneficial in maintaining good mental health. As our emotional intelligence increases, so too can our self-awareness and ability to regulate our emotions, which can help us respond to stressful situations in a more adaptive way. For example, with greater emotional intelligence, we can acknowledge when we are feeling overwhelmed rather than denying it or blaming others. With this increased self-awareness, we can adjust our environment (e.g., taking a break from work, speaking with a friend) or behavior (e.g., going for a run to clear our thoughts, engaging in mindfulness activities) in order to better manage the situation. Consequently, this could lead to more positive mental health outcomes, such as decreased stress and anxiety, greater feelings of resilience, and better relationships with those around us.

Emotional Intelligence and How It Impacts Your Social Life

From everything you've gathered so far, you might already know that having a high level of emotional intelligence is a key factor in forming connections and maintaining positive social relationships. Research has shown that emotional intelligence is strongly linked to successful social interactions, including the ability to foster productive relationships, support team members, empathize with colleagues, and expand one's social network (Lopes et al., 2004). In short, developing and utilizing your emotional intelligence can have a significant impact on the health of your social life as well.

When you are emotionally intelligent, you have greater awareness of your own feelings and the emotions of those around you. This heightened understanding will enable you to identify the needs and expectations of certain people and situations. Consequently, you are also better able to respond to these emotional needs and expectations with sensitivity and a more profound insight. This will allow you to take a more proactive step to strengthening your relationships. For example, you might find yourself in situations where you need to resolve conflict. After all, conflict is inevitable, especially when you lump together a group of people with varying perspectives. When you have high emotional intelligence, you are better able to manage this conflict so that it is productive instead of toxic. Emotional intelligence allows you to stay composed and calm as you navigate fiery emotions within the group in order to come to a meaningful resolution. As a result, you are often equipped to handle difficult dealings and conversations while also building fulfilling connections with the people around you. Also, emotional intelligence allows you to use empathy and attentiveness to be kinder to the people around you. This will enable them to be more comfortable around you as they give you a higher level of trust, support, and understanding.

Overall, research has shown that people who are emotionally intelligent are better equipped to move between different social circles, form meaningful connections, demonstrate empathy, and resolve conflicts (Lopes et al., 2004). Furthermore, developing your emotional intelligence can help create networks of relationships that are more productive and harmonious, contributing to a more positive overall social life.

Tips for Improving Your Emotional Intelligence

As we've reiterated over and over again, emotional intelligence is a skill that you can actively work on. Kids go to school in order to improve their IQ. They take classes and other academic pursuits in order to learn more about the world and improve their skill set. It's the same with EQ. Just because the skill doesn't seem *natural* to you doesn't mean that you can't develop it. To close out this chapter, we are going to go over some of the best tips that are designed to help you improve your emotional intelligence as you go through life.

Practice Mindfulness

Mindfulness is the practice of focusing on the present moment. Incorporate moments of mindfulness throughout your day to help you gain awareness of your current thoughts, feelings, and behaviors. For example, take a few minutes at the beginning or end of your day to sit in stillness and to observe and accept your emotions.

Practice Self-Compassion

Being kind and understanding in the face of your own failures can be a powerful tool in improving your emotional intelligence. Self-compassion involves recognizing when life gets difficult, offering yourself kindness and understanding, and recognizing you're not alone in your struggles. For instance, if you don't accomplish something you set out to do, don't be hard on yourself. Instead, offer yourself some positive support and encouragement to move forward.

Take Responsibility for Your Emotions

Taking responsibility for your own emotions can give you more control over how you experience them. Don't blame your feelings on others. Take the time to better understand why you're feeling a certain way and what you can do to manage and cope. To practice this, consider a hypothetical situation wherein your partner does something that irks you. Before unloading a wave of rage upon them, calm yourself first and try to acknowledge your feelings. Is the reason that you're upset really because of something that they've done? Or is it just because you're having a bad day in general, and your partner just happened to be the tipping point? In that case, do they really deserve for you to rage on them? Will that solve anything? Acknowledge that your emotional state is something that you can control and always take responsibility for how you act in emotional situations.

Change Perspective

Step outside of your emotions and take a look at a situation from a different point of view. Doing so can help you to better understand why others act or feel a certain way, as well as give you more control over your own emotions. If you're feeling angry or frustrated because someone close to you only offers criticism, try to understand why they may be reacting this way. Put yourself in their shoes and see where they're coming from. There could be many reasons why someone might always offer criticism. Perhaps they have a very critical or perfectionistic personality and find it difficult to offer positive feedback. Alternatively, they may feel frustrated or resentful about something in the relationship and are using criticism as a way to express their feelings. It's important to try to understand where the person is coming from and have an open and honest conversation to address any underlying issues.

Identify Common Triggers

Reflect and identify the things that consistently bring up negative emotions for you. Knowing what triggers negative emotions can help you better manage and cope with them. For example, if you've identified being stuck in traffic as a common trigger for your anger, come up with a plan for how you can manage this emotion in such situations.

Don't Take Things Personally

Now, this is a lot easier said than done, but try not to take things personally in daily situations. If you can better acknowledge that other people's reactions and emotions are based on their own outlook on life, it may be easier to separate your own emotional reactions and reactions from those of others. A classic situation wherein you can apply this is when your boss gives you a difficult task; remind yourself they're simply expecting you to do your job professionally and that it's not something that you should take personally.

Foster Emotional Awareness

Strengthen your emotional awareness by taking the time to focus internally and reflect on how and why you feel certain emotions. This can help you learn more about the source of the emotion and better equip yourself to manage it. For instance, if you're anxious about an upcoming presentation, spend some time recognizing the reasons why you may be feeling this way. By addressing your emotions head-on, you put yourself in a better position of being able to manage them effectively.

Communicate in an Authentic Manner

Improve your emotional intelligence by speaking about what you're feeling and thinking in an unambiguous and honest manner. Allow yourself to communicate openly without fear of judgment or criticism. There will always be times when you're feeling overwhelmed at work. Whenever that's the case, tell your supervisor how you're feeling and discuss how workloads can be amended. There's no reason for you to hide your emotions, especially when you know that you have so much to benefit from being honest with yourself and others.

Address Negative Thinking

To help keep your emotions in check, practice expressing positive emotions right after negative ones. Doing so can help to prevent negativity from accumulating and contributing to more intense negative emotions. Let's say that you are an avid golfer and you've just played a round of golf, and you know that you didn't perform your best. Rather than fixate on the bad game, try to focus on the few times when you were actually able to hit some good shots. Doing so will allow you to have a more positive disposition with the game and will prevent you from letting your negative thoughts take over.

Take Breaks Whenever Necessary

Make sure you're taking the time to care for your mental and emotional well-being. When emotions start to take over and become overwhelming, take a step back and take a break. For example, if you're feeling anxious or angry, step away from your desk and take a walk while practicing some mindful breathing. Even doing something as simple as that can go a long way in helping you to regulate your emotions better.

Get Enough Sleep

Ensure you're getting enough sleep, as sleep can have a significant impact on emotions and cognition. Getting quality rest can help to regulate your emotions and make it easier to manage them during the day. To get better sleep, before going to bed at night, avoid using screens and stimulating yourself with late-night activities.

Seek Professional Help When Necessary

It's normal to need help when it comes to understanding and managing emotions. If emotions become overwhelming or difficult to manage, seek help from a mental health professional. A professional can help you reflect on emotions in an objective way and help you identify healthier responses. It's always important that you understand that there's absolutely nothing wrong with wanting to deal with your issues with the help of a trained professional. Doing so requires a lot of honesty, bravery, and humility, all of which are admirable traits.

Make an Effort to Connect With Others

Spend time with the people around you who make you happy and who you can rely on for support. Doing so can strengthen your emotional intelligence, as it can provide you with insight into other people's emotions and help you better manage yours. For example, if a friend is sad, ask them how they're feeling and take the time to listen and offer them your support. Putting in the extra effort by involving yourself in these kinds of situations can definitely help you improve your emotional intelligence over time.

Exercise Regularly

Finally, make some time to exercise. You may not realize that exercise is essential to well-being and emotional intelligence. Regular physical activity can boost your mood, help you to better manage emotions, and strengthen skills like focus, patience, and self-control. To get the benefits of exercise, make sure to take time out of your day to practice some kind of physical activity; anything from a short walk or a full workout routine will be beneficial.

Chapter 3:

Positive Psychology

The notion of positive psychology has become a prominent feature of mental health interventions in recent years, as it focuses on building psychological resilience and increasing an individual's longevity of positive mental states. It has advanced mental health services by promoting well-being and improving quality of life for those with less severe mental health issues. In this chapter, we will explore positive psychology and its application in facilitating mental health and well-being. We will look at positive psychology interventions and explore the evidence behind them and their relevance and effectiveness in promoting good mental health.

First, we will explain how positive psychology has developed as a field of study and as an approach to mental health interventions. We will consider the theories and approaches adopted by the founders of positive psychology, the implications of their work, and how it has grown over the years in terms of its scope and application in interventions for mental health. We will also look at some of the different types of positive psychological interventions that have been used in mental health promotion and treatment, such as cognitive behavioral therapy, positive reinforcement, mindfulness-based approaches, and self-care. Then, this chapter will examine how each of these interventions can be used to help individuals with mental health issues, explore the evidence in favor of them, and discuss some of the criticisms they have received.

Naturally, this chapter will also touch on the impact of positive psychology on mental health by examining how it can help to reduce psychological distress, improve psychological well-being, and promote quality of life. We will consider how positive psychology can assist in the treatment of mental health issues, such as depression, anxiety, and low self-esteem, and how it can also be used to reduce the risk of relapse and promote emotional resilience. From there, we will discuss the potential benefits of these approaches on emotional regulation and self-reflection and how it encourages individuals to take more control of their emotional responses and behaviors.

Overall, this chapter will offer a deep exploration of positive psychology as a mental health intervention and how it factors into promoting good mental health.

Positive Psychology as a Traditional Mental Health Intervention

Positive psychology is an area of psychology that focuses on a person's strengths, abilities, and positive aspects of life rather than their weaknesses and struggles. With regard to its relation to promoting mental health, positive psychology takes a holistic approach when looking at the individual's mood, motivation, resilience, and well-being as a whole. Taking an encouraging, strength-based approach to mental health provides those at risk with a greater sense of self-efficacy and well-being.

Again, positive psychology is a field that emphasizes personal strengths rather than deficiencies. It focuses on helping individuals develop positive attitudes about themselves and promote positive resources for coping with life's demands. It looks at components such as optimism, gratitude, personal values and thoughts, and social skills. Moreover, it can provide positive interventions for treating various mental health conditions such as depression, anxiety, and PTSD.

When performed correctly, positive psychology strategies, such as positive affirmations, reframing, and savoring, can help you cope with difficult emotions and stresses that may arise from a mental health condition. Positive affirmations essentially involve repeating positive "self-talk" to yourself on a regular basis as a way to reduce negative thinking and build self-confidence. Reframing helps you to restructure negative thoughts into healthier cognitive responses that are less emotionally taxing. Finally, savoring is a tool to acknowledge and enjoy positive experiences to maximize their potential effects.

Positive psychology has become increasingly important in the field of mental health as it provides a holistic view to help you build the skills and strategies necessary to manage your mental health effectively. By cultivating personal strengths and exploring positive qualities, you can increase your sense of meaning and purpose, as well as your satisfaction in life overall.

One report mentioned that 85% of studies in the field have found that positive psychology has positive effects on psychological well-being, life satisfaction, and overall happiness (Hobbs et al., 2022).

Positive Psychology Interventions for Mental Health (and How to Apply Them)

Positive psychology interventions (PPIs) are methods of therapy that focus on building positive emotions and behaviors. These types of therapy encourage people to take an active role in improving their overall well-being by utilizing both cognitive and behavioral strategies. These interventions focus on building resilience, improving relationships, and fostering positive affect. Examples of PPIs include mindfulness techniques, self-care strategies, and gratitude exercises. These techniques have been shown to have a positive effect on mental health, stress, and overall well-being.

Gratitude Letters

Writing a grateful letter is a powerful process that can significantly boost happiness and well-being. Taking some time each day or week to think about someone you appreciate and write them a letter expressing your gratitude for their presence in your life. Alternatively, you can use a gratitude diary or journal to list out all the things that you are grateful for each day. This exercise requires you to reflect on the positive aspects and experiences of your life, thus helping to increase your overall happiness and well-being.

Daily Strength Awareness

The daily strength awareness (DSA) positive psychology intervention is a form of CBT that focuses on helping individuals increase self-awareness and a positive attitude toward life. This intervention is based on the idea that you can improve your own mental health by focusing on your strengths. DSA helps you identify your personal strengths, take action based on your strengths, and use them to achieve life goals. It also involves encouraging you to take positive actions and build resilience in the face of adversity. Additionally, DSA teaches techniques to manage negative thought patterns that can exacerbate depression and other forms of mental illness. By helping you shift your focus to your strengths and focus on achieving life goals, DSA encourages you to live your best life.

Mindfulness Meditation

Mindful meditation is an effective mindfulness tool that can help reduce stress and enhance well-being. Mindfulness meditation encourages you to concentrate on the present moment and let go of stressors and worries. Through mindful meditation, you can learn to identify your thoughts, better understand your emotions, and live in the present. Regular practice and reflection during the session can help strengthen your capacity to manage your emotions and foster a greater sense of well-being.

Reasonable Goal-Setting

Setting reasonable goals is a great way to stay motivated and achieve personal growth. Goal-setting is an important positive psychology intervention because it helps create energy and inspiration toward what you want to accomplish. Goals can help you tap into your internal strengths and talents, which enables you to progress toward your desired outcomes. Setting achievable goals can also help increase happiness levels; attaining a goal can feel like a great personal achievement.

Best Possible Self

We can also refer to the best possible self intervention as the self-reinforcement intervention. Self-reinforcement is an important strategy that fosters personal growth by recognizing, validating, and rewarding personal progress. When you identify and celebrate your successes, it encourages further motivation and courage. Whether written down in a personal journal or verbally acknowledged by peers, self-reinforcement allows you to have a greater appreciation for your accomplishments, thus creating overall improved levels of psychological well-being. You're constantly chasing after your best possible self and validating your efforts along the way.

Understanding Positive Psychotherapy

Positive psychotherapy is an evidence-based approach to mental health and well-being that focuses on an individual's strengths and their capacity to build upon those strengths. This form of psychotherapy uses a positive psychological framework to identify, foster, and maintain positive mental states, characteristics, and behaviors with the ultimate goal of increased well-being and happiness. This approach differs from traditional psychotherapy in that it deals with both the challenges and opportunities for growth for individuals, couples, and families. Positive psychotherapy also aims to understand a person's difficulties not simply from a problem-focused perspective but from the perspective of possibilities and potentials.

In comparison to positive psychology, positive psychotherapy is a more targeted approach that takes the concepts of positive psychology and applies them to individuals in a therapeutic setting. Whereas positive psychology applies the principles of positive psychology to a larger population, positive psychotherapy takes these principles, tailors them to the individual, and creates an evidence-based plan to help the individual achieve their goals and increase their well-being.

Practicing Gratitude

One of the interventions used in positive psychotherapy is the practice of gratitude. Gratitude is the practice of recognizing, appreciating, and expressing thanks for the good things in life. Practicing gratitude has been linked to improved physical and psychological health outcomes and increased life satisfaction.

Practicing gratitude can involve reflecting on the positive aspects of your life, being thankful for them, and expressing gratitude to others. For example, you could write a gratitude journal each day in which you list a few things you are grateful for. This encourages you to recognize the positive aspects of your life as well as the support you receive from others. It also serves as a reminder of the positive experiences you have had throughout your life. You can also express gratitude to others by writing them a thank-you note or thanking them directly. Doing this can not only strengthen relationships and lead to better health outcomes for the recipient (through the well-known phenomenon of "helper's high"), but it can also make you feel better about yourself for recognizing the positive aspects of their life.

Practicing Forgiveness

Practicing forgiveness can be explained as the act of intentionally releasing feelings of hostility and resentment and shifting one's perspective toward understanding and compassion. It is typically used to help people heal from the emotional and psychological pain caused by negative experiences or relationships.

As an example, a person might be struggling to move forward in their life after suffering a traumatic experience involving a past lover who had misled and betrayed them. The practice of forgiveness can be effective in overcoming the lingering, negative emotions associated with the event. It allows the person to recognize that the transgression was not intentional and to forgive the offender so that they can accept the situation, heal, and move on.

If this kind of situation applies to you, then you can start the process of forgiveness by acknowledging the hurt and negative feelings, allowing yourself to feel and express anger, sadness, and frustration, before beginning the process of letting go. To do this effectively, you need to consciously emphasize your understanding of the situation and the other person's behavior and focus on developing empathy, compassion, and kindness toward yourself and the other person. Then you can create a statement that expresses the intention of forgiving, such as "I am ready to forgive my ex-lover for hurting me, and I wish them well."

Finally, the last step is completing the gesture of releasing the anger, resentment, and pain you may have been holding on to while knowing you are working toward a more peaceful and positive way of living. Practicing this regularly, even just once a day, can help to make balanced feelings of empathy, respect, and understanding more accessible and easier to express. Over time, this practice can help you to foster a healthier emotional and psychological state, which will allow you to be in a better place to move on to a healthier and happier life.

Practicing Empathy

Practicing empathy is a positive psychotherapy intervention that involves actively engaging with and understanding the thoughts, emotions, and experiences of another person. It involves putting yourself in another person's shoes and seeing their perspective rather than just understanding the situation from your own viewpoint.

For example, if a friend is struggling with a loss, practicing empathy means listening without judgment and trying to understand the feelings and experiences of the person, such as loss or grief. This involves listening, validating, and recognizing the difficult situation they are in as well as appreciating their unique situation. It also includes providing emotional support and comfort.

Understanding the PERMA Model

The PERMA model was developed by Martin Seligman, a psychology professor at the University of Pennsylvania. It is a mental-health model based on positive psychology, and it stands for positive emotion, engagement, relationships, meaning, and accomplishments. The model's goal is to encourage individuals to become more mindful of their own happiness, recognize the resources available to them, and use those resources to their fullest potential.

The PERMA model was developed in 2011 when Seligman first proposed his Positive Psychology Intervention System (PPIS), an intervention based on the five elements of PERMA. Seligman believed that by incorporating these components into everyday life, individuals could lead more meaningful and rewarding lives.

Positive Emotion

Positive emotion is an important part of our overall well-being, giving us a sense of purpose, connection, and motivation to keep pursuing goals. It encourages people to focus on the happy, optimistic parts of life rather than the negative aspects. This particular component makes us feel good in the moment and can also improve our overall well-being by increasing our resilience to stress, which helps us take on challenges, improve our self-esteem, and enrich our relationships. Positive emotion can also lead to improved physical health by reducing stress hormones and increasing our immune system's capacity to ward off illness. In short, positive emotion is a vital component to achieving optimal mental health and well-being.

Engagement

Engagement refers to being actively involved in activities and pursuits that are meaningful and enjoyable. It can be manifested in the act of taking part in meaningful activities that are fulfilling and make you feel like part of a larger community. Contrary to popular belief, engagement is not just about having fun or doing enjoyable activities; it involves participating, connecting, and becoming engaged with a meaningful purpose. This can mean engaging in activities that allow you to grow and develop in meaningful ways. It is not just about activities that bring pleasure but also activities that allow you to contribute to something larger than yourself. Examples of such activities include volunteering, making art, collaborating on projects, or engaging in meaningful conversations.

Relationships

Relationships involve forming, sustaining, and enjoying positive connections with other people. They refer to the social connections and bonds we have with other people. They can be familial, romantic, platonic, or professional. Relationships always involve a dynamic of both give and take, reciprocity, and mutual respect. Mutual respect is when two people empower one another and recognize the strengths of each other. In order to have a healthy relationship, it is important to give and receive unconditional acceptance, understanding, support, and love. Additionally, relationships should be built on effective communication, trust, and honesty. Having relationships that are meaningful, secure, and satisfying also positively impact our well-being. Being a part of a strong supportive network can contribute to feelings of belonging, reduce feelings of loneliness, and help us get through hard times. Also, having positive relationships with others can lead to increased confidence and self-esteem.

Meaning

Meaning involves finding a sense of purpose or belonging in life, as well as a connection to the universe that transcends individual experience. It is the search for answers to life questions, such as "What is my purpose?" and "What matters in life?" Finding meaning in life can lead to a greater sense of satisfaction and well-being as well as having a positive effect on mental and physical health. Activities such as volunteering, spending time with friends and family, engaging in creative pursuits, or connecting with religious or spiritual beliefs can bring meaning to life. Taking the time to reflect and discover the things that are most important to you and the legacy that you want to leave behind can also contribute to a sense of meaning in life.

Accomplishments

Accomplishments refer to tangible results from making a difference in the world in meaningful ways. Accomplishments also lead to increased self-esteem, something that is closely related to happiness, an integral aspect of the PERMA model. Accomplishments come in various forms from completing an important project or goal to an individual achieving something meaningful in their lives, such as graduating college or completing a marathon. Accomplishments not only bring a sense of satisfaction, but they can also lead to greater goal attainment, which is a quality closely related to success and happiness.

In addition, accomplishments can be based upon personal development and growth. This could be something as simple as learning a new skill or habit or taking the time to build healthy relationships with others. By setting personal goals and striving to accomplish those goals, individuals are able to feel a greater sense of purpose and satisfaction in their lives. Furthermore, accomplishments can also translate into tangible rewards and goals achieved, such as a raise or promotion.

The ultimate goal of the PERMA model is to help boost mental health and overall happiness. Seligman's research has shown that practitioners of the PERMA model, who focus on cultivating the five elements of the model in their daily lives, tend to be happier, healthier, and more content than those who don't. Additionally, they tend to have improved social connections, better physical and mental health, and increased resilience, productivity, and success. By understanding and implementing the PERMA model, you can take tangible and meaningful steps toward creating the life you want.

Pros and Cons of Positive Psychology

In terms of understanding the value of positive psychology, it's important to have a holistic perspective on how this can impact a person's life. Of course, there are certain advantages to positive psychology, but there are some potential drawbacks as well. In this segment of the chapter, we will go over some of the pros and cons of positive psychology.

Pro: Encourages Growth and Fulfillment

Individuals who focus on positive emotions, rather than those that are negative or destructive, tend to be more resilient in the face of adversity.

By practicing such positive activities, individuals can maintain a greater sense of calm and satisfaction and cope better with stress. Positive psychology can help foster a greater sense of self-development, which in turn can lead to increased job satisfaction and better overall performance in the workplace. Also, positive psychology encourages the development of relationships. By engaging with and valuing the relationships we have with family and friends, we can increase our sense of well-being and connection to those we care about. This, again, helps to foster personal growth and satisfaction.

Con: Not Always Effective for Everyone

Positive psychology seeks to actively promote and cultivate positive emotions, experiences, and states of being. Though it has been largely successful in empirically helping individuals increase their happiness and life satisfaction, it is not always effective for everyone. The main reason why positive psychology is not always effective for everyone is because it does not take into account the full range of human emotion and experience. It assumes that individuals should strive for positive attitudes and focus on the positive aspects of life in order to feel better. However, this approach may not be effective for people who are dealing with unresolved emotions such as fear and anger. Additionally, some people may feel disconnected from the positive psychology concepts, which could further inhibit their potential to benefit from the practice.

Pro: Puts an Emphasis on Happiness and Well-Being

Positive psychology concentrates on building strengths and connecting with sources of happiness and well-being rather than dwelling on deficiencies and problems. The idea behind it is that if we focus on improving the positive outcomes, then we can create a healthier and more productive environment. Positive psychology looks to promote meaningful life engagement, thereby helping people to use the gifts and assets they already have.

Con: Disregards the Benefits of Experiencing Negative Emotions

In its approach to well-being, positive psychology disregards the benefits that may come from experiencing negative emotions. The idea is that negative emotions lead to a decrease in well-being and can often lead to negative behavior and outcomes. Therefore, the focus is more on cultivating positive emotions, such as gratitude, joy, and love, as opposed to focusing on and analyzing the negative emotions that may arise in a given situation. Some people have unresolved feelings and traumas that can't be addressed when they choose to stay positive all the time. You might have issues in the past that you won't be able to resolve if you just choose to focus on the positive.

Pro: Offers Opportunities for Constructive Problem-Solving

Through positive psychology, you gain insight into your own strengths, build resilience, and put those qualities to work in goal-directed problem-solving. Positive psychology encourages the development of self-efficacy, which gives you the confidence that you can solve problems independently and move forward in a meaningful way. Positive psychology also focuses on the promotion of self-awareness, an in-depth exploration of your thoughts, feelings, and values. By recognizing what motivates and inspires you, you are better able to take steps that can lead to effective problem-solving. Ultimately, positive psychology encourages you to focus on solutions, rather than problems, and teaches you to use reflective thought processes to explore alternative ways of thinking and acting in order to create solutions.

Con: Potentially Encourages Selfishness and Insensitivity

As you know, positive psychology emphasizes topics such as happiness, growth, and resilience and strives to create a more balanced and meaningful life. Although this approach can have some valuable and lasting benefits, it can also lead to a warped sense of reality and encourage selfishness and insensitivity. Focusing solely on positive emotions and experiences can lead to an attitude of indifference and disregard for the suffering of others.

The romanticization of positive thoughts, experiences, and emotions can lead to a false sense of security and an unrealistic expectation of happiness. Without the experience of more complex emotions, people can feel overwhelmed and out of their depth when difficult circumstances arise. This can lead to an inability to cope and excessive reliance on external sources of comfort, such as substances and escape behaviors.

Finally, positive psychology can also create a sense of entitlement. People may become overly focused on their own needs and feelings and believe that they deserve to feel happy and fulfilled all the time. Without looking at the world objectively, it is easy to reject the idea that there are problems that need to be solved and instead act in a self-serving manner. This can lead to a lack of meaningful contributions and ultimately a deep sense of disconnect from the world.

How Realistic Is Focusing on the Positive?

Positive psychology has long been used as a way to promote mental health and well-being. However, there can be potential pitfalls in its application that can lead to unrealistic expectations and beliefs. Some people may feel pressured to always have positive attitudes and think positive thoughts, irrespective of their current emotional state or reality. This can lead to feelings of guilt when these expectations are not met or can make someone feel like they are not "doing it right." Additionally, positive psychology can focus on the individual in a way that places too much of a burden on the self. People may believe that if they are not constantly positive and doing the "right" things that they are weak or a failure. This can lead to even more stress and anxiety.

This is where positive realism comes in.

Positive realism is a theory that was developed by psychologist Dr. Martin Seligman and is based on the idea that happiness is not a simplistic concept; it is a complex web of influences that make up a person's view of the world. This theory takes an optimistic view of life while also recognizing that adverse events and difficult times happen. Positive realism encourages individuals to take responsibility for the quality of their lives, stressing the importance of cognitive flexibility, personal growth, and behavioral change in order to create more positive outcomes.

Positive realism focuses on the present moment and encourages individuals to take active steps to make their lives more meaningful. It also focuses on creating a balance between pleasure and suffering, as well as finding meaning in both positive and negative life experiences. Positive realism helps individuals recognize the importance of managing their emotions in order to lead a happier and more fulfilling life.

It's believed that positive realism helps to make positive psychology more practical and realistic by presenting a balanced approach to life. It promotes the idea that we can create our own happiness and that it's not necessarily dependent on society or external factors. By recognizing both the good and the bad, we can develop resilience and use our emotions to manage difficult life situations and create more positive outcomes. This helps us become more independent and better equipped to handle life's challenges.

Tips for Nurturing Happiness

Sometimes, happiness can elude us. That's just being realistic. During hard or tumultuous times, it's always important that we make an effort to manufacture happiness in as organic and sustainable a manner as possible. That way we are better equipped to combat the harsh realities of everyday life. To close out this chapter, we are going to talk about some practical tips that you can employ to manufacture and nurture happiness in your own life.

Practice Gratitude

You may have heard the phrase "counting your blessings" and wondered what that has to do with happiness. Practicing gratitude is a fundamental part of a happy life and can help you nurture your happiness. When you focus on the things that bring you joy, whether it's your family, health, friends, or favorite hobbies, you can combat negative thoughts and feelings and stay productive and positive. Acknowledge the good things in your life, no matter how small they seem, and remember that they are what matter the most. Integrating gratitude into your day-to-day routine will help you in practical ways, such as allowing you to appreciate what is right in your life instead of worrying about what is lacking. You can even take a few moments each day to jot down things that you are thankful for. This will give you a better understanding of how much good there is in your life and put your worries in perspective.

Meditate

Another potential way to help nurture happiness is through meditation. Meditation is an effective way to relax your body and mind and be still for a period of time. It helps you to focus on your breathing and become more conscious of your thoughts and feelings. This, in turn, helps to reduce stress and anxiety and promotes feelings of inner peace. When you meditate, you become aware of your current state of happiness and identify areas that you can work on to increase it. You can also use meditation to clear your mind and let go of anxious thoughts or worries that may be weighing you down. With regular practice, it can help you to realize that the outer world is not responsible for your happiness, but instead you have the power to create it within yourself. Consistent meditation can also lead to improved self-awareness and an increased sense of connectedness with the world around you. When you become more conscious of your thoughts and feelings, you can start to become more mindful of your decisions and the effects those decisions will have on your own happiness.

Exercise

Exercising can be a great way to nurture happiness in your life. When you exercise, you release endorphins, which are hormones that can trigger a positive feeling in the body. When endorphins are released during exercise, you'll likely experience a sense of joy and satisfaction, reducing feelings of stress and anxiety. This is why exercises like running, jogging, riding a bike, or swimming can be so beneficial. Spending time exercising can also be a great way to reduce stress after a long day and can even help you get a better night's sleep, which we'll talk about later on. Additionally, exercise can help you keep your body healthy, making you feel better both physically and mentally. A regular exercise routine can also provide structure, which is important for feeling motivated and inspired.

Socialize

Socializing can be one of the best ways to nurture your own happiness. Spending time with others can help you make strong and meaningful connections with people who can provide you with emotional and social support. Engaging with people in meaningful conversation can give you the opportunity to reflect on what's really important to you in life or just to simply chat and laugh. Through hearing and sharing stories, ideas, and opinions, you can gain an interesting new perspective on life and experience new possibilities. So, getting out and connecting with others can be an important way to nurture your own happiness. Fostering relationships, spending quality time with friends, and engaging in meaningful conversations can help you to appreciate your own self-worth and feel connected to your community.

Connect With Nature

Connecting with nature can play a huge role in nurturing your happiness. It's one of the best ways to reconnect with yourself and appreciate the beauty in the world around you. When you spend time outdoors, you open yourself to the beauty of the landscape that's presented to you. You allow yourself to experience the sights and sounds around you and create a sense of peace in that moment. You can also take in the fresh air, which can improve oxygen levels in your body and reduce stress hormone levels. Appreciation for the beauty of the outdoors can be a great way to relieve stress and regain a sense of inner peace. Getting outside can also help you stay physically active, which, as we've already mentioned, is important for your overall health and well-being. Walking around a park, lake, or woods and exploring a trail are great ways to explore and get in some physical activity. This can help boost your mood and give you more energy.

Get Enough Quality Sleep

Who doesn't love a good night's sleep? When you're not getting enough sleep, you're more likely to feel irritable and stressed out. The lack of sleep can disrupt your ability to focus and make decisions throughout the day, which can cause major disruption to your happiness. A good night's sleep allows your brain to reset and prepare for the next day. When you sleep, the body repairs tissue, releases hormones, and can normally regulate the hormones that create happiness, such as serotonin. When you get enough quality sleep, it allows your body to perform all of these functions. Additionally, sleep helps with emotional regulation. When your emotional state is regulated, it allows you to have more positive emotions, perspective, and problem-solving abilities. You're better able to handle emotional issues, connect with people, and communicate effectively. All of these things are necessary for feelings of contentment and happiness.

Listen to Music

If you're feeling down or need a pick-me-up, listening to music can be a great way to nurture happiness. Music can have an incredible influence on our moods and emotions, so it's an excellent tool if you're looking to promote a more positive outlook and happiness. Listening to music that makes you feel good is an easy and effective way to lift your spirits. Choose tunes that make you smile, recall pleasant memories, or simply make you feel happy. You can listen to music with meaningful lyrics, uplifting beats, or simply something that gets your head nodding. It doesn't matter what type of music it is as long as it puts you in a good mood. Listening to music can also distract you from negative aspects of your life. Turn up the volume and then focus on the sound rather than your worries or anxieties.

Challenge Negative Thinking

You have probably experienced negative thinking at some point in your life—those doubts and insecurities that can stop you in your tracks and prevent you from pursuing your goals. Luckily, challenging negative thinking can help you to nurture happiness and move forward. The first step in challenging negative thinking is to become aware of when you're entering into a negative thought spiral. When you recognize that it's happening, focus your attention on the current moment. Become aware of your senses and the environment around you. Ground yourself in the present. Once you're in the present moment, you can start actively challenging your negative thoughts. Begin by questioning the reality behind your thoughts. Is it true that you're not good enough? Is this thought reasonable? Is it based on concrete evidence or just an assumption? By understanding the real issue behind your negative thoughts, you can implement a more positive solution.

Volunteer

You might not realize it, but getting involved in volunteering can be a great way to nurture happiness. Volunteering can help bring you out of your head, shift your perspective, and make you feel more connected to the people around you. When you're volunteering, you might find that you don't have time to be distracted by your own worries. You get to focus on something positive rather than on negative thoughts. Whether you're building a playground, donating time to a food pantry, or helping animals find new homes, your contributions matter and can bring purpose to your day. Also, when you're out there helping others, you can meet more people and participate in activities that make your community a better place. This could be a great opportunity to gain a greater understanding of the different types of people and cultures in your area.

Take Time to Relax and Unwind

When you give yourself the time and space to relax, you can breathe, slow down, and let go of any stressful or overwhelming feelings. Taking a break from your daily routine helps you to declutter your mind so that it is more naturally able to come up with ideas and solutions to challenges you face. Taking the time to relax and unwind helps you to be more mindful of yourself and your environment so that you can savor the moment and just feel the joy of being alive. It also helps you to be in the moment instead of worrying about what's going to happen in the future or dwelling on the mistakes of the past. Relaxation can also provide a great opportunity for you to connect with yourself and reconnect with the people that matter most in your life. When you're relaxed, you're in a better position to appreciate what's going well in your life, to show compassion and understanding to the people around you, and to make decisions that reflect your values.

Chapter 4:

Dialectical Behavior Therapy

When you first picked up this book, you were told that you would be able to significantly improve your mental health as a result of DBT. For the past three chapters, I've laid the foundation of everything you need to know about how your mental health works and the principles behind proven mental health techniques. For the rest of the book, I will be taking a more practical approach to discussing these concepts. The remaining chapters will teach you important concepts that are designed to help you take a more active role in promoting your own mental health. For this chapter, in particular, we will be focusing on what DBT is and how it can be effective for you. As you work through the following chapters, you will take the time to learn more about how to set your goals on your mental health journey and how you can practice mindfulness at all points throughout the process. After all, when you're constantly looking forward, it can be easy to disregard the present moment.

Ultimately, the goal of this chapter is to orient you on this new path that you're taking. We've already discussed a lot of the theoretical frameworks and mindsets that you need to learn in the previous chapters. Now it's time to take that first actual step to bettering your mental health and becoming the person that you deserve to be.

What Is DBT?

Dialectical behavior therapy (DBT) is a type of cognitive-behavioral therapy developed in the late 1980s by psychologist Marsha Linehan, PhD, of the University of Washington. It is a psychotherapy approach that emphasizes the psychosocial aspects of treatment while also incorporating skills from several other types of therapies, including mindfulness, distress tolerance, and behaviorism. The goal of DBT is to help an individual increase their personal awareness and acceptance of thoughts, feelings, and behaviors, while at the same time learning how to manage and eliminate distressing and/or maladaptive behaviors.

At its core, DBT is a form of interpersonal psychotherapy in which individuals learn to resolve conflicts and powerfully transform their lives. By bringing together the strengths of acceptance, change, problem-solving, and mindfulness, DBT seeks to empower people to work through their struggles and reach their therapy goals. DBT focuses on four main modules: mindfulness, distress tolerance, emotion regulation, and interpersonal effectiveness. Mindfulness focuses on being present in the moment without judgment or attachment to the current situation. Distress tolerance teaches positive coping skills, such as how to practice relaxation during intense moments of distress. Emotion regulation encourages the utilization of healthy coping mechanisms in order to become less reactive and more capable of responding. Interpersonal effectiveness focuses on developing effective communication skills and learning how to be assertive in social situations.

Through the modules, DBT is centered around helping individuals create meaningful connections with others by teaching skills that are necessary to help manage distress in difficult situations. Through the therapeutic process, individuals learn how to become their own best advocate and understand how to make conscious choices that are mindful and productive; this allows them to have lives that are more meaningful and have greater potential for lasting joy and fulfillment.

How Effective Is DBT for Improved Mental Health?

The best way to assess the effectiveness of DBT is to approach the concept on various levels. First, there is the emotional level. The skills of emotional regulation in DBT teach individuals to recognize and identify the emotion they are feeling and then to decide how to respond to them in a healthy and adaptive way. This includes teaching individuals how to identify their automatic thoughts in the moment and then how to challenge and modify these thoughts to help regulate their emotional responses.

On an interpersonal level, DBT helps the individual practice conscious communication, problem solving, and healthy relationships. This can include role-play exercises and skills for developing empathy and understanding. Interpersonal effectiveness skills help individuals develop the tools to communicate their needs and handle relationships with confidence and assertiveness. These skills help individuals effectively communicate their needs and be clear about the boundaries they have in their relationships.

On a behavioral level, DBT teaches the individual to recognize triggers of certain situations, develop new behaviors, and aim for a more positive lifestyle. This can include developing cognitive skills such as problem-solving and working toward individual values and goals. DBT could also potentially help individuals control and avoid self-destructive behaviors that compromise their overall mental health.

Generally, the effects of DBT can be quite powerful and long-lasting. As a result, it has been found to be one of the most effective treatments for a wide range of mental health issues including eating disorders, substance abuse, depression, and PTSD. Studies have found that DBT can reduce symptoms, help build self-esteem, increase interpersonal effectiveness, improve emotional regulation, and even reduce the risk of self-harm or suicide. It can also help the individual cope with difficult or stressful situations, develop positive relationships, and draw closer to an overall sense of purpose.

Starting Out: Setting Goals

When it comes to practicing DBT, there is an emphasis on having clear, achievable goals that you are actively working toward. This allows you to focus on making progress toward your goals instead of simply struggling to stay afloat. Setting specific, measurable goals that you can break down into smaller steps makes it easier to stay motivated and keep track of the progress you're making.

Goals provide a pathway to help you understand what you want to work on, what positive changes you would like to make, and how you will measure your progress. They offer focus and structure, giving you a clear idea of what you are working toward.

Having goals will help you stay focused and accountable throughout the therapeutic process, which allows you to set realistic expectations for your progress. Goals help to keep the focus on measurable outcomes rather than unhelpful and unattainable goals, such as, "I want to be happy all the time." DBT goals are often small, concrete, and achievable and help to provide direction for progress.

Additionally, goals can help you to stay motivated during times of frustration or disappointment when it can be difficult to stay focused on the ultimate aim. Setting parameters around your goals can be beneficial when it comes to staying motivated and committed to treatment. For example, if a goal is to reduce the amount of times you feel triggered, setting a measurable goal such as "I will practice mindfulness skills at least once a day" can help to keep you engaged and on track.

Another benefit to setting goals is that they can help to provide meaning and purpose to your treatment; by understanding the end goal or overall target, it can be easier to understand the individual steps and tasks needed to reach that target. Clear goals also help to provide a structure for therapy sessions and can be used to evaluate progress and make course corrections when necessary.

So how do you go about setting goals before starting DBT? Start by writing down your overall goals and then break them down into smaller steps. For example, if your overall goal is to learn how to cope with triggers, you might want to list out specific coping skills you want to work on as well as triggers you want to prepare for. You also should think about how you want to measure your progress. Are there certain behaviors or situations you want to avoid? Are there new skills or activities you want to be able to do or accomplish?

Once you have your specific, measurable goals set, you can start putting them into action. For example, if one of your goals is to learn how to manage your anger, make a list of the skills you plan to use, such as deep breathing, mindfulness, and cognitive restructuring. Each day you can practice these (or other) skills and track your progress.By setting goals before starting DBT, you can keep track of your progress, have something to aim for, and feel motivated to keep going. Whenever you feel lost in the goal-setting process, the following are a few tips that can help keep you on track.

Make sure your goal has two aspects: reachable, long-term objectives as well as shorter-term, achievable milestones. This will allow you to measure and track your progress and give you a powerful sense of accomplishment as you move forward. Next, always set goals that are SMART: specific, measurable, attainable, relevant, and time-bound. This will help ensure that your goals are realistic and relevant to the specific situation. Also, it's very important that you establish goals that are compatible with the long-term vision of where you want to be. DBT's focus is on lasting change, so be sure that your goals support that overarching goal. Finally, don't be afraid to reevaluate and readjust your goals to make sure they remain achievable. Don't be afraid to adjust course if necessary.

What is Mindfulness?

Mindfulness is a key concept of DBT and is used to help individuals develop awareness of emotions and behaviors, increase self-control, and improve communication skills. It is a practice of deliberately focusing your attention on the present moment. It is about being aware of your thoughts, feelings, and body sensations in a nonjudgmental way. The practice fosters a present-moment awareness that can help us be more aware of our own thoughts, emotions, and behaviors. It can help us maintain a certain level of clarity and calm while we go through life's experiences. With practice, mindfulness helps us become better at noticing the subtle changes in our mental state that can occur over time and taking proactive steps to make changes to improve our well-being. It also cultivates our ability to help separate what is happening in the present moment from past experiences that shaped our beliefs and values.

It is important to understand that mindfulness is not about being perfect, and it is not about suppressing or eliminating unpleasant thoughts or feelings. It is about being mindful of our thoughts and feelings and learning to observe them without judgment or reactions. It encourages the practice of being in the present moment, observing and accepting our thoughts and feelings as they come, and then letting them go. Mindfulness can be used in many areas of life, including relationships, work, and school. It can help us calm our minds when faced with stress, recognize our body's needs so that we can be more aware of our physical health, and develop a greater sense of self-compassion.

Within DBT, mindfulness can be used to teach emotion regulation. It helps you become aware of your current emotional state and understand why that emotion occurs. It then helps you learn the skills needed to manage your reaction to those emotions in a healthy and effective manner and choose a more beneficial response. Mindfulness can also help you better manage your interpersonal relationships. While it helps build awareness of your own triggers, it also helps you better recognize when your interactions with others are becoming unhealthy or dangerous. Through mindfulness, you can also learn healthy communication skills and learn how to better listen and respond non-defensively.

Overall, mindfulness is an important part of DBT and provides individuals with the tools needed to become aware of and better manage their thoughts, feelings, and behaviors. This improved awareness can help individuals make better decisions and develop healthy, sustainable relationships with those around them.

The Six Core Mindfulness Skills

The six mindfulness skills of DBT offer individuals the opportunity to change their thoughts and behaviors so they can live with more peace and purpose. These skills help people focus on the present moment, become aware of their thoughts and feelings, and manage their emotions in a healthier way. By consistently practicing these six mindfulness skills, individuals can create greater self-awareness and regulate their emotions more effectively. In this section, we will explore the six mindfulness skills of DBT and the potential benefits of implementing them into your daily life.

Observing

This skill involves learning to notice and be aware of thoughts, feelings, and physical sensations without any judgment or getting caught up in them. This helps to reduce the amount of mental and emotional clutter and enhances your ability to take action in the moment. It also gives you the space to be mindful and practice self-compassion.

Describing

By describing your thoughts and feelings, you can gain insight into your inner life. This allows for a deeper understanding of your emotional experiences and allows us to be more connected to our emotions and more patient when dealing with them. This skill also helps us to cope with strong emotions and make better decisions.

Participating

Participating is an essential part of mindfulness in DBT and refers to actively engaging in an experience by fully immersing in it. Participating is different from simply observing or describing the experience because it involves taking part in it, which can provide clarity and help identify patterns and habits. Participating encourages you to become present in the present moment and accept that it is what is, without trying to change it in any way.

Non-Judging

Being non-judging is the practice of viewing situations in an objective and compassionate way. It is the intuitive capacity to understand a situation and make decisions based on what is right for you in that moment. As mindfulness practitioners, we can cultivate a non-judgmental Wise Mind by attending to all experiences without assigning "good" or "bad" labels. This skill helps you observe yourself and the world around you more objectively.

One-Mindfully

This skill involves the practice of calmly focusing on one thing at a time. This can include being able to concentrate on a specific activity or task, being present in a conversation, or being more mindful of your environment. By practicing one-mindfulness, you can be more present and connected to your experience and remain focused on the task at hand.

Effectiveness

Finally, there is the skill of pursuing effectiveness. This skill involves setting realistic goals and taking actions that are likely to lead to desired outcomes. This skill can help you have a better understanding of your skills and abilities, develop problem-solving strategies for challenging scenarios, and make informed decisions that are likely to have successful results.

How to Practice Mindfulness

The practice of mindfulness has become increasingly popular in recent years, with an emphasis on being present and aware of our thoughts, feelings, and environment. Mindfulness can be applied in almost any situation, from our work to our relationships, and even in moments of stress or difficulty. It is an effective tool for enhancing well-being, improving relationships, increasing focus and productivity, and coping with stress. This section of the book will discuss the different ways that mindfulness can be practiced in various settings and how it can be beneficial in our daily lives.

When Waking up to Start the Day

Mindfulness is a great way to start your day with intention. Practicing mindfulness when you first wake up can set the tone of the day and make it easier to stay present and in tune with yourself. To practice mindfulness when waking up, start by lying in bed in whatever position is comfortable for you. Take a few deep breaths, focusing on the feeling of your breath as it moves in and out of your body. Take note of any sounds, smells, or sensations occurring around you. Analyze how you are feeling physically, mentally, and emotionally. Then turn your attention to a single bodily sensation such as the bed on your back or your hand on the sheets. Feel each sensation as deeply as possible and simply observe with kindness any thoughts that arise in your mind. Acknowledge each thought without judging or analyzing and simply let them pass. When you're finished, take a few more deep breaths and slowly open your eyes. This practice can help you start the day feeling focused, connected with yourself, and more mindful of the present moment.

When Stressed With Work

Mindfulness is also an effective way of reducing stress and gaining clarity in difficult situations. When working, it is important to be aware of the present moment and practice staying in tune with both your internal and external environments. To do this, start with focusing on your breath. Taking deep, even breaths and then releasing them slowly can help to create a sense of calm and prevent panic or overwhelming feelings. Next, look around and become aware of what's around you. Notice the sensations, sounds, and smells, and then let your awareness slowly move inward to your body. Feel the sensation of your body in the chair or standing in your space. Acknowledge any feelings that come up without judging or analyzing them. When your mind starts to wander, take a deep breath and return your attention to the present. Mindfulness can be practiced in small moments throughout the day. Each time you check your phone or take a break, try to be mindful and bring your focus back to the present. Doing this can help to reduce stress and allow for clarity and productivity. Additionally, it can help provide insight about how to best approach the task or project at hand.

When Eating

Practicing mindfulness while eating can be incredibly beneficial and help in developing a healthier relationship with food as well as help to recognize the signs of fullness earlier and reduce overeating. A great way to practice mindfulness when eating is to start by bringing your awareness to the present moment. Notice the space you're in, the physical sensations in your body, and your breath, and then start to tune into the experience of eating. Slow down and take the time to really tune into the flavors, textures, and smells of your food by savoring each bite. Notice how your mind starts to wander and steadily bring your focus and awareness back to the present. With practice, mindful eating can help you become more mindful of your satiety and better attuned to when you feel satisfied and no longer hungry. When you find yourself becoming distracted by thoughts or feeling overwhelmed, just take a few moments to pause, refocus your awareness, and bring your attention back to the present.

When Exercising or Working Out

Mindfulness is an important practice to help increase focus and enhance your workout. With mindful exercising, you allow yourself to become more aware of your body during your workout, which allows for increased energy and improved performance. To practice mindfulness during your workout, start by finding a comfortable, quiet place with minimal distractions. Take a few moments to focus on your breathing and allow your body to relax. Once relaxed, focus on how your body moves during each exercise and how you feel when you complete each set. Notice how your muscles contract and stretch, as well as how your breathing changes. During the workout, pay attention to your thoughts. Be aware of your emotions and physical sensations; allow them to fuel your workout. If you feel yourself becoming too distracted with outside thoughts, refocus your attention back to your body, the movements you're making, and how you feel. Finally, end your workout with some deep breaths and a few moments of reflection on your performance. Celebrate and notice the changes within your body and mind. Over time, mindfulness will not only help you reach greater heights with your fitness but will also lead to a better understanding of yourself and your capabilities.

When Driving

When driving, it is important to practice mindfulness to stay present, focused, and safe. To begin, set an intention to remain mindful during your drive. Take a deep breath in and out and remind yourself to stay attentive and aware. As you drive, notice the beauty of your surroundings and the other drivers around you. Pay attention to your emotional and physical experience, being sure to take a few deep breaths and stay calm when you catch yourself feeling tense or negative. Listen to the sound of the engine and the road. Notice the pressure of the gas pedal underneath your foot and the motion of your hands as you hold the steering wheel. Strive to be aware of everything that's happening around you and give your full attention to the task of driving. Take time to notice the road signs and adjustments that you need to make as you drive. When your mind inevitably wanders, observe the thoughts and feelings that come up, notice how they feel in your body, then gently return your focus back to the act of driving. In this way, you can practice mindfulness while driving, staying alert and in tune with the moment.

When Socializing

Practicing mindfulness when socializing can help create more meaningful conversations and connections with others. The key is to be present and to listen intently in the moment to what the other person is saying. Create a comfortable and relaxed atmosphere. Find a quiet space that allows you to focus on the conversation and take a few deep breaths to center yourself before starting. Then, try to focus on the present moment and tune out any potential distractions. Instead of focusing on the end of the conversation or the task or errand that you have to do later, remain present and listen closely and with genuine interest. Once you find your mind wandering, practice some grounding techniques to refocus your attention. Focus on your breath or the physical sensations in your body to bring yourself back to the present moment. Also, let go of any need to control the conversation and be patient with yourself if you can't think of the perfect reply. Really listen and think about the other person's words before responding. Finally, be kind to yourself. We all make mistakes and experience awkward conversations. If you find yourself in an uncomfortable situation, be gentle with yourself and remember that practice leads to improvement over time.

When Overthinking

When you start to feel overwhelmed by your thoughts, the first step is to slow down and practice deep breathing. Close your eyes and focus your attention on your breath. Take slow, deep breaths and feel the sensation of the air entering and leaving your body. If this doesn't help, you can try progressive muscle relaxation, which involves tensing and releasing different muscle groups. Another tip is to focus on the five senses. Witness the sights and sounds around you; take in the smells, taste, and sensations of your body and environment. Focusing on the senses shifts your attention away from the thoughts and helps you stay grounded in the present moment. With regular practice, you will become more familiar with mindfulness and will be better able to handle your overthinking.

When Preparing for Sleep

Mindfulness is a powerful tool that can be used to help relax and prepare for a good night's sleep. To practice mindfulness prior to going to bed, start by making sure your bedroom is quiet and comfortable. Dim the lights, if possible. Lie down on your bed and take a few deep breaths. Close your eyes and begin to focus on your breathing. Pay attention to the rhythm of your inhales and exhales. Allow your body to relax and any excessive tension to dissipate. Observe any thoughts that cross your mind without judgment or commentary and let them pass swiftly by. If your mind wanders off, take notice of that and gently direct it back to your breath. By doing this you will come to recognize that some days our minds may be more settled than other days. After several minutes of mindfulness, gradually release your awareness and take a few more deep breaths. Allow your body to mold into the mattress and let yourself drift off into a peaceful, restful sleep.

Chapter 5:

Interpersonal Effectiveness

For this phase of your DBT journey, we will learn all about how to develop interpersonal effectiveness. At the end of the day, your mental health isn't just reliant on your inner thoughts and dealings. A lot of it is also influenced by how you deal with other people in your life. The quality of your relationships, especially with the people that you spend a lot of time with, can greatly impact the state of your mental health. That's precisely why this chapter is going to be dedicated to a particular skill that's crucial to improving your capacities for socialization and relationship-building—interpersonal effectiveness.

Interpersonal effectiveness is the ability to effectively manage relationships and communication with people. It involves developing a range of skills such as communication, assertiveness, decision-making, problem-solving, and conflict resolution to navigate interpersonal challenges. Interpersonal effectiveness is important for developing positive and meaningful relationships with others, being able to influence people in a positive way, and managing the stress associated with interpersonal relationships.

Being able to communicate and interact effectively with other people is key to success in both professional and personal relationships. It involves being able to use appropriate language and maintain appropriate body language, listen actively, and establish an environment of mutual respect. People with effective interpersonal skills are better able to give and receive feedback as well as handle difficult conversations with different personality types. Aside from that, the ability to make decisions, solve problems, and manage conflict is also an important part of being an effective communicator. Being able to assess situations, identify potential consequences, and weigh the pros and cons of different options for resolving conflicts or reaching a decision is important for interpersonal success.

Overall, interpersonal effectiveness is an important skill for having positive relationships and managing stress in both personal and professional settings. It involves developing skills such as communication, decision-making, problem-solving, assertiveness, and conflict resolution to effectively interact and communicate with others. Due to its importance, every effort should be made to strengthen interpersonal effectiveness at whatever stage of life.

Interpersonal Effectiveness in DBT: Mental Health Meets Social Health

Developing social skills and interpersonal relationships is one of the most important aspects of DBT. This is because social skills and interpersonal relationships provide an essential platform for improving mental health, as well as providing support and developing a sense of self-worth. Social skills enable us to interact and communicate with others. They allow us to exist in a society that values collaboration, cohabitation, and teamwork. This is important in understanding how people experience and interact with the world and how to respond or react to certain situations. Interpersonal relationships act as the foundation for developing a sense of community and providing emotional support to those involved.

Interpersonal relationships also influence our overall well-being and mental health. Having meaningful connections with people can reduce feelings of isolation and loneliness, as well as provide comfort and companionship when needed. Furthermore, when we have positive relationships, it can contribute to our sense of self-esteem and identity, as this can have a ripple effect in improving our overall mood and attitude. In DBT, developing social skills and interpersonal relationships is often used to help individuals better manage difficult thoughts and emotions, as well as find coping mechanisms that can help them build resilience and competency. Ultimately, building strong and nurturing relationships is essential in our lives, not only because it helps us to understand and empathize with others, but also because it can benefit our own mental health and well-being.

Interpersonal effectiveness is a key pillar of DBT. This type of behavior therapy focuses on developing skills to help individuals decrease distress as well as improve overall functioning in their personal and professional lives. Interpersonal effectiveness skills help individuals navigate interpersonal interactions and relationships by providing guidelines for approaching relationships from an assertive and mindful attitude. Some of these skills taught through DBT include the ability to effectively communicate, listen, and problem-solve. It teaches individuals to be open-minded and respectful of others while dealing with conflicts, set boundaries, protect oneself, and stay away from people who are not beneficial.

These skills enable us to more confidently and effectively manage our relationships and day-to-day interactions as well as increase our self-esteem and sense of worth. Improving social skills is also important to developing interpersonal effectiveness because we need to be able to properly read other people's reactions, understand body language, and manage conversations. This combination of techniques is essential to providing a framework for effective and assertive communication in any interpersonal situation. The overall goal of interpersonal effectiveness is to promote healthy and assertive communication between individuals, leading to improved personal relationships and increased self-awareness.

Interpersonal Effectiveness Skills That You Need

Interpersonal effectiveness skills are fundamental in many aspects of our lives and can have a dramatic impact on our overall sense of well-being, self-esteem, and career success. In this section of the book, we will explore the various interpersonal effectiveness skills you need to develop to be successful in your personal relationships, professional lives, and other areas of life. So whether you are looking to build new relationships or strengthen existing ones, these skills will act as the tools you need to become a more effective communicator and get the most out of your relationships.

Active Listening

Active listening is a term used to describe a particular type of listening that is focused on understanding the speaker rather than just hearing their words. This form of listening requires the listener to listen carefully, retain information, ask questions, and take time to acknowledge what they have heard. It has been found to be an effective tool for building relationships as it allows the listener to better understand the speaker's perspective, gain insight into issues they may be struggling with, and build trust and respect. Active listening encourages empathy, which is key to building a strong relationship.

As an active listener, you should make an effort to suspend judgment and be open-minded to all points of view. You should focus on understanding the speaker's message and not on any preconceived notions you might have. Active listening involves paying close attention to body language and facial expressions to help better understand the speaker.

Empathy

Empathy is the ability to recognize, understand, and share the feelings of another person. It is the capacity to take on the emotional perspective of another person and to respond with understanding and compassion. Empathy is an important skill that can help build better relationships because it allows us to better understand how others feel and what they may be experiencing. When we demonstrate empathy to someone, we are showing them that we are understanding and supportive. This can help create a sense of safety, trust, and connection, which is essential to strong, healthy relationships.

When communicating with another person, using empathy can go a long way in forming meaningful connections. Empathy helps us foster a sense of trust, respect, and understanding by listening closely to what the other person is saying and conveying a sense of compassion and support. It allows us to truly see the other person's perspective, rather than our own, and to appreciate and acknowledge their feelings. When we demonstrate empathy in our interactions, we show the other person that we are sensitive and caring, which is a key ingredient for building better relationships.

Conflict Resolution

Conflict resolution is the process of resolving a dispute or disagreement by coming to a mutually acceptable solution. It involves social and emotional skills such as negotiation, mediation, arbitration, and problem solving. This skill helps to build better relationships by allowing parties involved in a dispute to talk out their differences, process the emotions involved, and come to a resolution that everyone is comfortable with. In essence, it is a form of communication in which everyone has a better understanding of one another, as well as a better understanding of the different perspectives at play. Conflict resolution promotes respect and understanding, which can lead to more harmonious relationships. For example, if two colleagues that don't get along are able to resolve their differences through constructive dialogue, they will not only be more productive, but they can grow to respect and trust one another more. Conflict resolution also helps those involved to better recognize their own behaviors and how they influence the disagreements they have with others. It may also help to reduce conflict in the future because people are less likely to feel attacked or misunderstood and therefore less likely to react defensively.

Collaboration

Collaboration is the skill of working together with one or more people to achieve a shared goal. The process of collaboration involves communication, creativity, problem-solving, and joint decision-making. Collaboration enables people to work together to accomplish greater results than if each person worked individually. When people collaborate, they share ideas and opinions, creating a pool of perspectives to draw from, which helps solve complex problems. Collaboration encourages positive communication, as ideas are shared openly between team members and feedback is exchanged.

Self-Regulation

Self-regulation is the ability to manage one's emotions, thoughts, and behaviors in a way that is constructive and beneficial to oneself and others. Self-regulation involves recognizing and monitoring one's own internal states—such as feelings, thoughts, physical sensations, and impulses—and being mindful of how these internal states affect one's external behavior in various situations. Through this awareness, you can develop skills to consciously manage your emotions, thoughts, and behaviors in order to produce desired outcomes, regardless of your initial emotional state.

The ability to regulate one's own emotions, thoughts, and behaviors in a positive and productive way is essential for forming and maintaining healthy and supportive relationships. People who are able to self-regulate are more likely to communicate and interact positively with others. You can more easily recognize and consider the feelings, thoughts, and needs of yourself as well as others before behaving in a manner that may be damaging to the relationship. As a result, you are better able to resolve conflicts, express and receive empathy, and create an overall atmosphere of respect and emotional safety.

Respectful Interaction

Respectful interaction is the ability to interact with others in a way that shows consideration and deference toward their feelings, perspectives, and beliefs. It involves being mindful of the words used, the tone of voice, body language, and the amount of personal space and attention given to the other person. Respectful interaction also involves active listening, which is engaging and responding to the other person with genuine care and interest. By showing respect to others, not only do you build stronger relationships with them, but you also gain their respect in return. Respectful interaction cultivates trust and understanding while reducing conflict and animosity. It overcomes animosity, encourages compromise, and creates an environment of trust where meaningful dialogue can occur. Ultimately, respectful interaction helps to foster more compassionate, honest, and meaningful relationships between people.

Think DEARMAN, GIVE, and FAST

Interpersonal effectiveness is not necessarily a skill that always comes naturally to certain people. That's why self-awareness and self-regulation are particularly important whenever you find yourself interacting with others. Whenever you feel like you're at a crossroads with regard to how you should be socializing with the people around you, don't forget to think DEARMAN, GIVE, and FAST. Don't know what that means? Let's break it down.

DEARMAN

The first thing you have to determine when you're interacting with a person is what you want to get out of that interaction. Any kind of interaction should have a sense of objectiveness about it so that it gives you a sense of purpose and fulfillment. In order for you to honestly and clearly express your needs in a social situation, make use of the DEARMAN acronym: describe, express, assert, reinforce, mindful, appear, negotiate.

The first step in using DEARMAN is to describe the situation to the other person without labeling or judging them. This helps the other person get a better understanding of your perspective.

After the situation has been described, the next step is to express your feelings about the situation. Letting the other person know how you feel about the situation is important in order to ensure honest and open communication.

Once you've expressed your feelings, the next step is to assert your needs and wants. Make sure to be clear and direct with what you're asking for and why you desire it.

After asking for what you need, it's important to reinforce your position and validate the other person's feelings, if applicable. For example, if you're asking a friend to complete a task that they've agreed to do, you can thank them for their commitment and remind them of the deadline.

Once you've reinforced your position, the next step is to stay mindful. This means stepping back and being aware of your own feelings. If the situation starts to escalate, take the time to check in with yourself, regain focus, and avoid knee-jerk reactions.

The next step in using DEARMAN is to appear confident. This means using a calm and assertive tone of voice when speaking, maintaining appropriate body language, and being respectful to the other person.

Finally, you have to learn how to negotiate in order to round out the DEARMAN approach. In negotiating, not everyone will agree with you. Listen to what others have to say. Be willing to make some adjustments and find solutions to the problem together.

By using DEARMAN in your interpersonal interactions, you can become more effective in communicating your needs and expressing yourself.

GIVE

GIVE is a strategy for interpersonal effectiveness that focuses on behaving gently, expressing genuine interest in the other person, validating their perspective, and avoiding pushiness. GIVE (gentle, interest, validate, easy) is mostly designed to help you foster more positive interactions.

Being gentle involves using a light, non-confrontational touch in conversations. Speak in a calm and relaxed manner, be understanding of each other's feelings, and avoid an aggressive tone.

Showing interest can be manifested through listening actively, asking questions, and communicating a genuine sense of care and concern. Being engaged in the conversation is the key to creating an equitable, respectful dialogue.

Next, you need to make an effort to validate a person by acknowledging and accepting their perspectives, especially when they differ from yours. Even if you disagree, recognize that they have a valid point of view, which may be based on their interpretation of the situation. Also, remind yourself that you aren't always right.

Finally, always be easy in your dealings with other people. Don't be difficult to socialize with. Take things slowly. People tend to be less defensive when they are allowed to arrive at their own conclusions. Don't be pushy or overly persuasive. Let the conversation unfold naturally and encourage discussion without pressure.

FAST

We also have to talk about what it means to value self-respect when interacting with others. At the end of the day, you want to foster better relationships with others, but it should never be at the expense of your principles and values. This is precisely where the acronym FAST (fair, apologies, stick to values, truthful) comes in.

Being fair means taking a clear, honest, and unbiased approach when discussing conflicts. It involves understanding the issue and trying to reach a solution that is beneficial for everyone involved while avoiding any kind of personal judgments and criticisms.

Next, it's important that you don't apologize unless it's warranted. You should never have to apologize for expressing an opinion, disagreeing with someone, or making a request. Understand that whenever you *do* apologize, it should not be seen as an admission of guilt. Rather, it is merely a sign of good communication and empathy.

Of course, in your dealings with others, you should also try to stick to your core values and not be swayed by emotions or fear. By adhering to your values, you can remain focused on the matter at hand and work toward a solution that everyone can agree on.

Finally, you should always stay truthful. This means staying honest, open, and transparent throughout the conversation. Misunderstandings and false assumptions can be avoided if everyone speaks the truth and communicates their feelings effectively. This can help to create an environment of trust and mutual understanding.

Benefits of Developing Interpersonal Effectiveness Skills

Before we close this chapter, it's important that we are able to reemphasize the value of developing your interpersonal effectiveness skills. As the old cliché goes, no man is an island. At the end of the day, you have to learn how to deal with others effectively in order for you to live a more meaningful and fulfilling life. In this section, we will discuss the benefits of developing interpersonal effectiveness skills in order to provide you with a more profound appreciation for them.

Improved Self-Confidence

Interpersonal effectiveness is a vital part of developing and maintaining self-confidence. By becoming more aware and intentional in our interactions, we can gain confidence in our ability to maintain and build relationships, express our emotions, and handle interpersonal conflict. This, in turn, improves our self-confidence. With better interpersonal effectiveness, we become more secure in our communication, clearer and more accurate in our self-expression, and more empowered to maintain and form relationships. This can allow us to form meaningful connections with others, which fosters a sense of purpose and self-assurance.

Enhanced Leadership Skills

Interpersonal effectiveness is a powerful tool that can help enhance any leader's skills. Leaders must be able to clearly communicate expectations and facilitate collaboration among groups of people. Through the use of effective interpersonal practices, leaders can foster greater trust, collaboration, and respect, resulting in higher productivity. Leaders must also be able to listen and respond thoughtfully to team members in order to understand their problems, as well as offer constructive feedback. Such skills also ensure that everyone in the team feels valuable, which is essential for any successful team.

Fruitful Collaborative Efforts

In any collaborative project, it is important to foster cooperative intentions. This can be achieved through empathy and constructive conversations and being comfortable enough to be open and honest. Engaging in active listening, asking questions, and being able to provide others with feedback allows for a more fruitful experience. Being able to recognize and manage any emotions related to the project, such as frustration and stress, and to take responsibility for any potential mistakes, can help to create a better working environment. All in all, utilizing interpersonal effectiveness principles in any collaborative effort can lead to positive results and a job well done. If a team is working efficiently, they are likely to develop better solutions faster and have a sense of satisfaction that their efforts have contributed to positive outcomes.

Increased Empathy and Understanding

Interpersonal effectiveness is an important skill that can help to increase empathy and understanding in relationships. This skill gives people the ability to communicate one's thoughts and feelings in a clear, assertive way and in a way that conveys respect for oneself and others. This allows communication to be more productive, as each person is understood and able to voice their concerns and opinions more clearly. It also encourages meaningful dialogue, which is essential for understanding different ideas and opinions.

Modulating Interpersonal Intensity

To finish this chapter, I will be talking about another important concept that relates to interpersonal effectiveness—interpersonal intensity. Interpersonal intensity is the level of intensity between two people when they interact. It reflects how closely and deeply they interact and communicate on an emotional, mental, and physical level. This intensity may vary depending on the situation and the type of relationship they have. Interpersonal intensity typically refers to the level of intensity between two people that has a direct impact on the quality of their relationship. It is often used to assess compatibility and depth of connection between two people.

Interpersonal intensity can be measured in many different ways. In romantic relationships, for example, it can be evaluated by assessing how passionately the couple expresses their feelings for each other, the degree of trust and respect, and the level of commitment. In platonic relationships, interpersonal intensity is demonstrated through shared interests, mutual appreciation, and communication. Interpersonal intensity is important in any kind of relationship, as it helps determine whether the relationship is healthy and successful.

Modulating interpersonal intensity is critical for successful interpersonal relationships. It is important to be able to gauge the appropriate level of intensity for a given relationship or situation. If a person is too intense or forceful, it can lead to angry and overwhelming feelings, while too little intensity can lead to a lack of passion or understanding. Being able to recognize the needs of the other person and adjust the intensity accordingly is essential for building trust and respect.

By modulating interpersonal intensity, one can ensure that everyone involved in a conversation feels heard and respected. Modulating interpersonal intensity also helps avoid potential conflict. When two people interact, they bring their own personalities, perspectives, and goals to the conversation. If one person is overly intense and the other is not, the conversation can quickly reach an impasse where both parties become frustrated, and individuals can feel ostracized or defensive.

You can modulate interpersonal intensity by first identifying your own personal level of intensity, which describes how intense you feel in a given situation. If your personal level of intensity is higher than the situation requires, it may be best to dial it back slightly in order to match the intensity of the conversation or social interaction. Conversely, if your personal level of intensity is lower than the situation requires, you may need to step up the energy to create positive, constructive interactions.

The next step is to assess the situation and those you are interacting with. Understanding the context and assessing the emotions of the people in the conversation or interaction can help you to adjust your intensity as needed. This can be done by reading the nonverbal and verbal cues and the overall tone of the conversation.

Once you have identified the other person's level of intensity and the situation, the next step is to modulate your own intensity level. This could include speaking more softly or slowly, using fewer hand gestures, or simply taking a few breaths and relaxing to calm down. If the situation calls for an increase in intensity, it may be useful to add more humor to the discussion, inject enthusiasm and energy into your voice, and use more hand gestures to emphasize your points.

Finally, it is important to remain aware of how your behaviors may be affecting the other person in the exchange. If the other person's level of intensity is dropping and they are seeking a more relaxed interaction, it is important to adjust your level of intensity and engagement accordingly.

Chapter 6:

Distress Tolerance

As you may already know, distress tolerance is a critical skill in many areas of life, including our psychological and emotional health. It encompasses the ability to cope with, and even overcome, distressing emotions and situations. However, it's also possible that you have no idea what distress tolerance actually is and just how significantly it can impact your life.

At its core, distress tolerance is about creating a sense of resilience to stressful events and external influences instead of letting them control our lives. Not only does this skill benefit us emotionally, but it enables us to take a more thoughtful approach to problem-solving. The practice of distress tolerance has now been integrated into DBT. Ultimately, DBT provides a structured and effective way to acquire, practice, and perfect distress tolerance skills, with an emphasis on learning to regulate emotions and tolerate distress.

This chapter will explore the role of distress tolerance in relation to DBT and how it can ultimately play an important role in your own mental and emotional formation. We look at how distress tolerance can be used to improve your mental health and well-being. Developing distress tolerance can be beneficial in overcoming a variety of stressful emotions and situations. By developing distress tolerance, you are able to remain in control of any situation you are in instead of quickly reacting and taking actions that may not lead to desired outcomes.

What Is Distress Tolerance?

Distress tolerance is the ability to accept and endure negative emotions, either internal or external, without trying to change them or make them go away. It is an important skill in learning to cope with adversity and tolerate difficult circumstances. It involves accepting difficult experiences and taking action to prevent them from having a greater negative effect on one's mental or emotional well-being.

Distress tolerance can help a person manage distress and difficult situations better. It teaches them how to remain calm and cope when faced with tension-inducing life situations. It helps them bear the emotional pain of anxiety, rejection, and failure. It also teaches them how to move past their distress instead of avoiding it and becoming overwhelmed. Distress tolerance can lead to an individual developing healthier coping strategies, feeling more in control of their emotions, and being better able to manage life events and setbacks. Furthermore, distress tolerance helps an individual settle disputes and argue in a civil and composed manner, reducing the negativity of any given situation.

To truly understand how distress tolerance can help a person, consider this hypothetical story of a man named Dylan. Dylan has recently been let go from his job and is feeling overwhelmed and anxious. He is unable to find any new opportunities and can't seem to escape from the cycle of feeling down and overwhelmed. Dylan's friends have been encouraging him to invest time and money in some stress-relief activities, such as yoga or meditation, but he's struggling to find any kind of motivation. In order to cope with this difficult time and at the advice of one insightful friend, Dylan decides to practice distress tolerance. After reading some books and articles about distress tolerance, Dylan tries integrating these principles into his daily life. He starts to recognize the feelings of stress and anxiety, but instead of trying to seek out immediate relief, he takes a step back and focuses on his current situation. He takes a few deep breaths and consciously uses the skills he has learned from his studies and readings. He decides to take a break from job-searching and dedicate some of his free time to reading a book, going for a walk, or engaging in an activity that he finds fulfilling, even if it's just a short break. He focuses on the activities that bring him joy, knowing that his job situation will improve, and he will be able to move on eventually. In the meantime, he is able to develop a healthier relationship with his stress and anxiety and maintain his well-being while he continues to search for new opportunities.

In that sense, Dylan didn't necessarily get rid of his stressors and problems. Rather, he shifted his perspective on his situation and his approach to dealing with these problems so that they weren't able to negatively affect him as much. This is exactly how developing distress tolerance can help you as well. It's not about living a problem-free life. It's about developing a mindset and disposition that allows you to stay sane and in control despite whatever problems come your way.

The Skills and Techniques of Distress Tolerance

This section of the book will focus on the various distress tolerance techniques that you can use to successfully manage stress and crises. We will be looking at different methods and strategies that can be utilized to effectively regulate emotions, manage stressful situations, and build emotional resilience. We will also be discussing ways in which individuals can learn to establish better coping skills for adverse situations and how to find a balanced approach to address distressing times. The main goal of this section is to provide you with the knowledge and understanding needed to make the best decisions to increase your emotional functioning in difficult moments or situations.

STOP

DBT's STOP skill is a technique used to help people manage difficult emotions and distress. The acronym stands for stop, take a step back, observe, and proceed mindfully. The main goal of this skill is to reduce the intensity of emotion and help control the impulses that often accompany intense emotions. STOP focuses on becoming aware of the current moment and allowing intense emotions to pass without acting on them. This helps to provide some space both emotionally and physically in order to give the person an option to choose a response instead of just reacting to the emotion.

Here are the basic steps to practice STOP:

1. Stop: Remind yourself to pause and take a step back. Take a few slow, calming breaths.

2. Take a step back: Notice that something is happening inside of you. Instead of identifying with the emotion, imagine that you are stepping outside of yourself and observing what is happening from a distance.

3. Observe: Identify the emotion and thoughts that are arising. Examine physical sensations that may accompany the emotion. Notice any judgments or comments about the emotion or yourself.

4. Proceed mindfully: With awareness and curiosity, consider the options you have in the situation. Notice potential consequences of different responses. Choose a response or action with the goal of practicing self-care and achieving a desirable outcome.

By practicing STOP and recognizing the options available during intense moments, you can learn to manage your emotions in healthy ways. This can help to reduce impulsivity and improve regulation of emotion, leading to better overall mental health.

TIPP

TIPP (temperature, intense exercise, paced breathing, and paired muscle relaxation) skills are a set of four strategies used in distress tolerance to manage distressing emotions and urges without resorting to maladaptive coping strategies. Temperature skills involve changing the temperature of a room or environment in order to alter the body's physiological arousal level. Intense exercise skills involve performing a few minutes of physical activity such as push-ups, jumping jacks, or running in place in order to increase endorphins, decrease arousal, and become aware of the body's physical sensations. Paced breathing skills involve breathing in a rhythmic and intentional way that is slow and deep to reduce physiological arousal. Finally, paired muscle relaxation is a relaxation technique involving tensing and releasing specific muscle groups in order to relax the entire body and reduce anxiety.

TIPP skills work to create new and healthy habits that can be used to manage distress in the long-term. When in a distressing emotional state, it can be difficult to think clearly and make the most adaptive choices. By learning these TIPP skills and employing them at those times, it can help to decrease the intensity of the current feeling in order to come up with a healthier and more adaptive solution.

Pros and Cons List

A pros and cons list is a distress tolerance skill used in DBT. It's used to help individuals learn how to make healthy, rational decisions when faced with difficult situations or emotions. This skill is especially helpful when quick decisions are required, yet the person is feeling overwhelmed or otherwise struggling in the moment.

To practice creating a pros and cons list, start by writing down the pros and cons of a particular situation. In the column labeled "pros," list all of the positive aspects of your situation. In the other column labeled "cons," list all of the difficulties or disadvantages of your situation. Once you've written out your list, review and compare each item. Think about how each factor could affect the outcome if you choose either to take action or not.

When making a decision based on your pros and cons list, try to look at it objectively without judging or exaggerating any details. Each item should be given equal weight. Identify positive and negative aspects of each choice and try to decide which is the best choice that will lead to the desired outcome. Doing a pros and cons list can also help you to minimize regret by assessing all the potential outcomes of each choice you make.

Practicing the pros and cons list in distress tolerance can help you become more aware of the consequences of your decisions and weigh the pros and cons of a particular situation in a thoughtful, balanced way. It is a powerful tool to help you make decisions in difficult or challenging moments, and it can be an effective way to manage your emotions when life becomes overwhelming.

Distracting

Distracting is an important skill in DBT for distress tolerance. This involves distracting oneself from an intense emotion or urge in order to reduce its intensity. The aim of distraction is not to deny or repress emotion but to take a break from it temporarily. This can help foster an attitude of acceptance so you can allow the emotions to exist without being overwhelmed by them.

Practicing the distracting skill can be done by exploring the world around you. This involves focusing on sensory experiences and physical sensations. You may explore sights, sounds, textures, tastes, and smells to distract from the intense emotion. You can also engage in creative activities such as drawing, painting, or playing a musical instrument as a distraction. Exercise and physical activities can also be used for distraction as long as it does not become traumatic. Additionally, you may explore novel activities such as reading a book, going on a hike, or learning a new skill. Engaging in meaningful conversations with friends or family members or just having a general social interaction can also be helpful for distracting.

IMPROVE

The IMPROVE (imagery, meaning, prayer, relaxation, one thing in the moment, vacation, and encouragement) skillset is a set of evidence-based skills used to manage distress and enhance emotional and psychological regulation. Developed through DBT, IMPROVE skills are used to aid individuals in tolerating distressful and uncomfortable emotions, urges, and events in a healthier and more productive way.

Imagery involves the usage of mental images and scenarios to aid in the visualization of future events, hopes, and goals. Imagery can help individuals gain a greater sense of control over their feelings, thoughts, and behaviors and to increase motivation for positive change.

Meaning involves the exploration of one's life and the understanding of what meaning can be taken from pain and suffering. This can be done through story-telling, journaling, and other forms of creative expression. Through the process of reflection, you can gain insight, hope, and a greater understanding of yourself.

Prayer means utilizing prayer, mindfulness, and sensory exploration to create a sense of peace and relaxation. Through the intentional use of prayer and personal reflection, individuals can become better grounded and centered.

Relaxation involves calming down the body and mind through the use of relaxation methods such as meditation, yoga, and other stress-reduction practices. Relaxation can help to reduce tension and emotional reactivity, which allows you to regain control of the situation.

One thing in the moment means focusing on one task in the present moment to stay grounded and relaxed. This can be anything from taking a few deep breaths to looking at a reminder of a hard-earned accomplishment. This helps to keep you focused, empowered, and present to whatever is happening.

Vacation means taking a break from intense emotions and situations. This can be done through breaks from work, time spent in nature, or through engaging in activities such as reading, listening to music, or anything that helps to create feelings of calm and relaxation.

Encouragement is the process of using positive statements and affirmations to help foster the courage and self-efficacy needed to succeed. This could include making a list of reasons why one deserves to succeed, telling oneself positive affirmations, or sharing positive stories of success with others.

By practicing the IMPROVE skills, you can develop the self-confidence and resilience to manage distress in healthier and more productive ways.

Self-Soothing

Self-soothing is another basic distress tolerance skill that's used in DBT. This practice helps to regulate intensely emotional states or negative thoughts that cause distress. Self-soothing is a way to soothe and calm yourself without indulging in potentially harmful behaviors. It helps to replace unhealthy coping strategies with healthy ones and to regulate intense emotions.

The self-soothing practice can be utilized in different ways. When feeling strong emotions such as anger, sadness, or agitation, it is important to identify the feeling and note if it is the result of a particular emotion, such as anger or sadness. Once the feeling is identified, proceed to connect to the body to take deep breaths and relax. This helps to reduce the intensity of the emotion by focusing the mind on something pleasant and calming.

Once the body is calmed and relaxed, other strategies for self-soothing can be used. This could include listening to soothing music, using aromatherapy, or engaging in some kind of distracting activity such as reading or playing a game. Additionally, focusing on positive self-talk or affirming words can also help to soothe you emotionally.

An essential aspect of self-soothing is the act of taking a break from a difficult emotion or situation. This could involve going outside, taking a walk, or opening up the windows in a room to refresh the environment. It is key to remember that you should not force the emotion or situation away but move away from it in order to be able to observe it in a less intense manner.

Radical Acceptance

Radical acceptance is a skill in DBT that encourages individuals to practice accepting their current situation or feelings, despite the desire to want to change them. It teaches individuals to accept reality and cognitively deny the impulse to escape it, as well as to develop meaningful values and goals instead of avoiding the experience. Radical acceptance is similar to mindfulness in the sense that it encourages individuals to acknowledge feelings without judgment or resistance. Rather than trying to change their emotional state, radical acceptance encourages individuals to validate and observe their emotional experience without feeling obligated to act on it.

Practicing radical acceptance involves allowing and accepting the present moment, as difficult as that may be. You will tell yourself, "This is what it is" instead of engaging in negative thoughts that may spiral into avoidance behaviors or further distress. It is important to remember that this does not equate to passivity. Rather, this allows the experience to exist without giving it more power than necessary. As a skill, radical acceptance must be implemented daily, even if it feels uncomfortable or awkward. It takes time for individuals to recognize that radical acceptance is not the same as giving up hope. While acknowledging current feelings, you must strive to value and shape your identity around meaningful goals instead of adaptive behaviors based in avoidance.

Paced Breathing

The paced breathing DBT skill for distress tolerance is a technique used to manage acute feelings of distress that can be difficult to regulate without proper preparation. This skill encourages you to become conscious of your body while utilizing mindful breathing methods to reduce anxiety and help exhibit greater self-control.

To practice paced breathing, you can begin by finding a comfortable and relaxed position that avoids physical tension. Close your eyes and focus on your breath, taking gradual and deep breaths. Once you have done this, inhale over the count of five seconds, then hold your breath for a count of one. After this, slowly exhale over the count of seven seconds and rest momentarily. Throughout each breath cycle, pay attention to how the body reacts and observe sensations that may come and pass. Repeat this cycle for five minutes or until desired relaxation is obtained. With practice, mindful and slow breathing cycles will become easier.

Alternate Rebellion

Finally, the alternate rebellion skill is one that teaches individuals to find healthy and productive ways of expressing their emotions and feelings. Rather than act out your distress in harmful ways, this skill teaches you to express your distress in a productive, healthy manner. Practicing the alternate rebellion DBT skill begins with identifying what kind of emotion is being felt and understanding it. Individuals should ask themselves why they are feeling the way they are. Once they have identified and understood their emotion, they should think of appropriate and healthy ways that they can express it. This could include writing a letter that they never send, walking away from a situation, or finding a friend to talk to. The idea is to find an emotion regulation approach that can be used to manage the emotion instead of using destructive behavior.

It is important to remember to stay mindful while practicing the alternate rebellion DBT skill and to be aware of how your emotions are influencing your decisions. This can help to ensure that your emotions are expressed in a way that is appropriate and productive. This skill can help you to be more mindful of your emotions and understand the importance of finding ways to cope with intense emotions. With practice, you can learn to develop a better understanding of your emotions and how to best manage them in uncomfortable situations.

Chapter 7:

Emotional Regulation

We're reaching the final stretch of this process of helping you achieve better mental health through DBT. To recap, in the first chapters, you oriented yourself on what DBT is and the role that mindfulness plays in that process. After that, you learned all about interpersonal effectiveness and the role that other people play in the formation of your mental health. Then you spent some time learning about distress tolerance and building yourself up to be someone who is able to withstand stressful situations. Before we proceed to the final phases of this process, it's important that you take the time to recognize just how far you've come and all of the progress that you've made. The work that you've done so far is definitely something that you shouldn't belittle or underestimate. You've done a great job, and you have all the momentum you need to keep on pushing forward, which brings us to the topic for this final chapter: emotional regulation.

In the world of mental health, emotional regulation is a key tool for both physical and psychological well-being. It is a process that assists individuals in managing their emotions as well as how they react to them. As a result, emotional regulation can be a valuable strategy for dealing with common life events, such as conflict and stress, as well as more serious issues, such as anxiety and depression. When used in the formulation of DBT, emotional regulation provides you with the skills necessary to understand and modify your patterns of behavior and psychological distress. This chapter will cover the fundamentals of emotional regulation, its relationship to DBT, and the various ways it can be used therapeutically. In doing so, we will explore the various elements of emotional regulation, as well as the various DBT skills that have been developed to teach people about regulation. Through this exploration, you can gain a better understanding of the idea of regulation, how it can affect well-being, and how it can be incorporated into a successful form of therapy.

We will begin with an overview of the basics of emotional regulation and the way it has been addressed in the field of psychology. We will then look at the various components that encompass emotional regulation, such as self-awareness, impulse control, and coping skills. These components, when put together, form the building blocks of effective regulation and form the basis of the DBT conversations. From there, we will delve deeper into how DBT encourages the use of skills and strategies to promote emotional regulation and addresses common issues that come up in therapy.

To conclude this chapter, I will offer concrete examples and practical strategies for incorporating emotional regulation into DBT and the associated benefits of doing so. By the end, I hope to have provided a comprehensive guide to understanding emotional regulation and how it can generate a significantly positive impact on your life.

Emotional Regulation vs Emotional Dysregulation

Emotional regulation is an important skill set mastered by many individuals. It is the ability to recognize, identify, and take action to cope with and manage one's emotions. Emotional regulation is a learned skill, but it can be improved with practice and understanding, just like many other skills and components in DBT. Ultimately, DBT is there to help you manage and regulate your emotions in healthy and helpful ways. Emotional regulation techniques used in DBT are diverse and include activities such as mindfulness, distraction, reframing, and social problem-solving. Each technique can be practiced independently to help you manage your emotions in the moment or used in conjunction with each other to create well-rounded strategies to regulate your feelings. We'll get more into the best emotional regulation practices and techniques later in the chapter. But for now, all you have to know is that as you practice emotional regulation skills in DBT, you will build resilience and become better able to cope with intense emotions. The goal is to be able to accurately identify, recognize, and manage excessive emotions in a healthy way, which can lead to increased self-confidence and improved quality of life.

Emotional regulation is also a practice of fighting against emotional dysregulation. This is a condition in which an individual has difficulty regulating their emotions. It involves experiencing intense and volatile feelings, an inability to manage or control them, and a tendency to react strongly in high-pressure situations. This difficulty in regulating emotions often leads to distress, impulsivity, and an inability to cope with life's challenges.

The underlying causes of emotional dysregulation can be complex and vary from person to person. Possible contributing factors could include unresolved trauma, a history of volatile or unstable relationships, and past experiences of neglect and abuse. Additionally, people are more prone to emotional dysregulation if they have inherited a tendency to be more emotionally reactive. Underlying neurological functions can also contribute to emotional dysregulation. Neurotransmitters—chemical messengers in the brain—play an important role in regulating emotions. They are responsible for transmitting signals between neurons in the brain that allow us to process and respond to external stimuli. If these connections become disrupted, it can lead to difficulty controlling emotions.

Another factor that contributes to emotional dysregulation is physical illness or substance abuse. When someone is dealing with an illness, the symptoms can cause a significant amount of physical and emotional discomfort. This can lead to an inability to control or understand emotions or to disordered thinking which can further exacerbate problems. Substance abuse can also disrupt the functions of neurotransmitters, leading to difficulty in regulating emotions.

This is precisely where emotional regulation techniques come in. The key to managing emotional dysregulation is to practice emotional regulation techniques on a regular basis. By focusing on understanding one's emotions, as well as making use of tools like mindfulness and positive self-talk, it is possible to gain better control over one's emotions and to use them to communicate more effectively with others. Additionally, surrounding oneself with a strong, supportive network can be an essential component in managing emotional dysregulation. With the right combination of techniques, individuals can learn to respond to challenging situations in a healthy and productive manner.

Getting in Touch With Your Emotions

Do you find yourself living life on autopilot and going through the motions without really acknowledging how you feel about anything? Maybe it's time to get in touch with your feelings. This can be a tricky process, and it's something that most of us struggle with. But with a bit of focus and attention, it's something that can be learned and practiced. In this section of the book, we're going to dive into the steps and tools necessary to understand and express your emotions. I'll talk about why it's important, explore different methods and activities, and provide you with tips and strategies to open up your emotional world.

Identify and Label Your Emotions

Identifying and labeling your emotions is a healthy practice because it allows you to gain greater awareness and understanding of your emotions and to learn how to respond in a productive way to them. The first step to identifying and labeling your emotions is recognizing and acknowledging that you are feeling something. It may help to keep a journal to note when you experience any emotional changes. Make sure to take note if you experience any physical sensations such as stomach tightness and nausea as these are indicators of emotion as well. The next step is to identify and name the emotion you are feeling. This can be a difficult process because we often confuse emotions and lump them together but having a better knowledge of each emotion can help.

Different emotions have their own individual characteristics, intensities, and duration. Some emotions may be linked to one another but try to separate them as best you can. The final step in this process is to take note of the context in which the emotion arose. Taking into account your unique situation, the environment, and how you were feeling before the emotion hit can provide you with a greater understanding of yourself.

Communicate Your Feelings Even When Difficult

Communicating your emotions is important even when it may be difficult. By learning to be more communicative and open about your feelings and reactions, you can create a deeper, more meaningful relationship with yourself and others. When it comes to expressing your emotions, the most important thing to remember is to be honest and authentic. Make sure that you're communicating how you truly feel, rather than what you think others would like to hear. If done in a healthy manner, it can help you to process your feelings and gain insight into yourself and your relationships.

Also, when communicating your feelings, choose your words carefully. Many people try to skirt around the issue by using passive phrases that don't directly express their true emotion. Instead of saying something like, "I think you should..." or "I don't like it when...", try to be more direct and specific with your language—"I feel frustrated when you do that," "I want..." or "I don't feel comfortable with...". Expressing your emotions can be difficult, but it is an important, ongoing process. By taking the time to learn to communicate your emotions in an honest and healthy way, you can foster deeper connections, gain greater insights into yourself, and create relationships of understanding and acceptance.

Channel Your Emotional Energy Into Something Healthy

The value of channeling negative emotional energy into something positive is two-fold. First, it releases stress, tension, and negative thoughts from your mind. This allows you to clear your head and focus more clearly on the task at hand. Second, it often leads to positive physical and emotional sensations that can lift your mood, help you experience more joy, and even increase your motivation and productivity. One way to channel negative emotional energy into something positive is to practice mindful meditation and relaxation. This involves focusing on your breathing and allowing yourself to be aware of your body and your thoughts. You can mentally release any negative energy or feelings of stress or tension. This can be especially helpful if you find yourself feeling stuck in a negative pattern of thinking. Another approach is to engage in activities that lift your mood. This could be anything from listening to music or dancing to laughing with friends or exercising. Finally, expressing your emotions through creative outlets such as writing, drawing, or painting can help to shift your energy and focus your attention on something more constructive and positive.

Don't Let Your Emotions Bottle up Without Any Resolution

When emotions are not expressed in some way, they can become "bottled up," meaning they are unable to be resolved and instead remain inside the person who is feeling them. Bottled-up emotions can be very dangerous because they can manifest in different ways such as poor physical health, mental issues such as depression or anxiety, and behavior issues such as acting out in some way.

If a person stops trying to take care of their physical health and avoid stress, they can become more vulnerable to illness. They can also become prone to overeating, which can cause weight gain and further health issues. Mentally, emotions that are not addressed can lead to depression and anxiety. Stifling emotions will lead to deep feelings of hopelessness, worthlessness, and lack of joy. Additionally, bottled-up emotions can lead to unhealthy thought and behavior patterns. Behaviorally, a person with unaddressed emotions may act out in ways that can be destructive to themselves and those around them. It is vital for you to find ways to talk about how you feel and find healthy outlets for the stress and pressure that come with emotions.

Understanding Primary and Secondary Emotions

Understanding your emotions is essential to making sure you have a healthy mind, but what are primary and secondary emotions? Primary emotions are the core feelings you experience throughout your life such as happiness, sadness, anger, fear, and disgust. Secondary emotions, also known as more complex emotions, include envy, empathy, pride, shame, and guilt. In this section of the chapter, we will take a closer look at these two types of emotions, exploring the characteristics that differentiate them and the different ways in which they can help us in our lives.

Primary emotions are the core feelings that humans experience in reaction to certain situations such as joy, anger, sadness, fear, surprise, disgust, and contempt. These emotions are associated with physiological reactions like sweating, increased heart rate, or blushing. They are considered to be basic human emotions because they are generally shared across cultures and are necessary for the development of secondary emotions.

Secondary emotions are emotions that are based on primary emotions and are usually influenced by cultural and environmental factors. Examples of secondary emotions include guilt, shame, pride, envy, and sympathy. These emotions are more complex than primary emotions and are often the result of an individual's perception of the situation.

The main difference between primary and secondary emotions is that primary emotions come from a basic physical response to a situation, while secondary emotions come from a more complex set of social and psychological factors. It is important to understand the difference between primary and secondary emotions because it can help you understand your own emotions and those of other people. Knowing the difference helps you make better decisions, as secondary emotions can be more dangerous and lead to irrational decisions. Additionally, understanding the difference between primary and secondary emotions can help you recognize how your emotions are being influenced by external factors, which allows you to better manage your emotions.

DBT Emotional Regulation Skills

Emotional regulation has become ever-important as mental health struggles seem to affect more people than ever before. With this in mind, DBT emotional regulation skills are a valuable tool in helping us to establish balance in our emotional lives. In this next section, we will discuss various DBT emotional regulation skills and how they can help us to effectively manage our emotional states and the associated behaviors.

Positive Self-Talk

Positive self-talk is a skill used in DBT to help you talk to yourself in a more positive and realistic light. It can be an effective way to cope with emotional crises as well as daily life stressors. Positive self-talk is a technique that involves talking to yourself using statements or images that are not only positive but also realistic. The idea is to counterbalance the negative, distorted, or unhelpful thoughts you may have in situations that may provoke such thoughts. You may find that engaging in positive self-talk can help you stay grounded and connected to reality. Positive self-talk might sound like, "I can get through this; I am strong," or "I can handle this situation, I am capable," etc. You may find it helpful to use different sentences or phrases in order to customize your self-talk. Ultimately, it helps to remind you of both the positive moments in life as well as your own personal strengths.

Opposite Action

Opposite action is a skill that involves using an action that is opposite of a natural, strong emotion. The goal of this skill is to replace an emotion like anger or sadness with a more balanced emotion like contentment or ease. This skill helps regulate emotions and lessen the intensity of strong emotions. To use the opposite action skill, start by identifying the emotion you are feeling in the moment. Once you have identified the emotion, such as sadness, think of an action that would be the opposite of that emotion. The point is to choose an action that forces your mind to focus on something else other than your emotion. For example, if you are feeling sad, then the opposite action may be to go for a walk outside or to start a conversation with someone. The activity that you choose should bring a sense of joy, peace, contentment or anything that is the opposite of the emotion you are feeling.

Another way to use opposite action is to think about how someone who feels the opposite of the emotion you are feeling might act and then do the same. For example, if you are feeling sad, think about how someone who is feeling joyful might act. They might smile, practice deep breathing, or talk to a friend. Doing these things can help distract you from your emotions and reduce the intensity.

ABC and PLEASE

The ABC skill can help you better manage your emotions. This skill is designed to direct people to establish healthy habits and behaviors that will allow them to better regulate emotions, thoughts, and behaviors. It can be broken down into three phases: accumulate positive emotions, build mastery, and cope ahead.

The accumulated positive emotional part of the skill helps you build your emotional resources by seizing the good moments in your life. Notice and take in any pleasurable experiences you have like spending time with loved ones or soaking up the beauty of nature. This will increase your emotional reserves and allow you to handle difficult situations better.

The build mastery portion is about learning to do something new or doing something better. Focus on skills that you want to improve or learn. Challenge yourself to do something new and build the confidence that comes with mastering something. You can also focus on reframing failures as chances to learn and grow.

The cope ahead part teaches you how to plan ahead to handle potential problems. Anticipate situations you might find challenging and identify strategies that can help you manage your emotions. It is also important to recognize any triggers that may lead to stressful situations so you can plan to avoid or manage them.

Practicing the ABC skill will help you build resilience and a better sense of well-being. Start noticing small, pleasant experiences, challenge yourself to do something new, and plan ahead to handle difficult situations. It takes practice, but with each step you take, you are closer to becoming the best version of yourself.

The PLEASE DBT skill is used to promote well-being in individuals who are struggling with emotional dysregulation or mental health issues. It was developed to support individuals in developing healthy coping mechanisms for managing chronic and acute stress. The concept of PLEASE emphasizes five components: physical illness, eating, avoiding mood-altering drugs, sleep, and exercise.

The physical illness component emphasizes the importance of attending to any physical illnesses or health concerns. It is essential to access any necessary medical care, including utilizing telemedicine, if possible.

Eating regular and healthy meals is essential for physical health, mental well-being, and overall stability. Eating healthy meals and snacks helps to maintain energy levels that may be depleted during times of stress.

Avoiding mood-altering drugs, alcohol, and nicotine to cope with stressful environments or situations is recommended as they can only provide a temporary and unreliable solution.

Getting adequate sleep is vital for physical health, mental health, and emotional regulation. When we don't get enough sleep, this can make it difficult to think clearly or stay in the present moment.

Incorporating exercise or other physical activity into your daily routine is essential for mental and physical well-being. Exercise promotes healthy sleep patterns, helps to reduce feelings of stress, and boosts confidence.

Strategies to Help You Regulate Your Emotions

Feeling overwhelmed by emotion can make it difficult to stay focused, make rational decisions, and prioritize your actions. When you feel overwhelmed by emotions, it can be hard to bring your attention back to the present moment. Fortunately, there are many strategies to help you regulate your emotions and bring peace and balance back into your life. In this section, we'll explore some of the top strategies to help you remain balanced and even-keeled when life gets overwhelming. From mindfulness techniques to physical activities, these are the tools you need to help you maintain emotional balance and achieve greater harmony in your life.

Force a Smile

Forcing a smile is a technique used to help regulate emotions. It is effective because the physical action of smiling can help cue the brain to produce serotonin, the "happiness" chemical. When the brain experiences a feeling of reward, it will begin to create positive chemical reactions in the body, leading to a feeling of well-being and improved mood. Additionally, research has shown that forcing a smile can actually cause the body to experience the physiological states associated with actually feeling happy (Spector, 2018). This means that even if a person is experiencing negative feelings, their body will still begin to physically relax, reducing the intensity of the emotion.

Get up and Move

Getting up and moving is an effective way to regulate emotions because it encourages the body to release hormones and neurochemicals that can have a calming effect on the mind. Exercise helps to reduce the intensity of your emotional reaction in several ways, including reducing the production of cortisol (which is the stress hormone), increasing the production of endorphins (which are hormones that are responsible for good feelings), and helping improve your overall mood. Physical activity can help to distract the mind from negative thoughts and emotions, allowing the person to focus on something else and shift their attention away from their emotional state. Finally, engaging in physical activity can also provide an emotional outlet by allowing the person to express their emotions and release built-up tension.

Do a Breathing Exercise

Breathing exercises are effective for emotional regulation due to the fact that they slow down the heart rate and relax the body. This allows you to move out of the fight or flight response and into a calmer state of mind. By taking slow and deep breaths, the body is able to relax the muscles, which helps decrease stress levels and take you out of a state of panic and into a more balanced and calmer mindset. This balance can help regulate emotions, allowing for better control over how you are feeling and thinking. Breathing exercises can provide a much-needed break from life's stressors and a sense of clarity and emotional stability. As you become aware of your breath, you can begin to direct your focus away from your worries and onto the breath in order to better manage your emotional state.

Analyze the Impact of Your Feelings

Analyzing the impact of your feelings can be an effective tool for emotional regulation because it provides a deeper understanding of how emotions affect you. It's through understanding the ways in which your emotions manifest and how they manifest wherein you can become more aware of your emotional state. This awareness provides you with the information you need to better recognize your emotional responses to situations as well as how your responses influence your behavior. Also, this enables you to identify patterns of emotional reactivity and learn how to respond to situations healthily instead of simply reacting impulsively.

Aim for Regulation Instead of Repression

Regulation refers to the ability to manage your emotional responses to an event or situation. This can involve strategies such as reframing a situation, using mindfulness techniques, journaling, or engaging in physical activities. It is important to regulate emotions because it helps to promote emotional health, resilience, and overall well-being. Repression refers to the internal process of denying or suppressing feelings or emotions. Repression is unhelpful for emotional regulation because it can lead to feelings of distress, depression, and anxiety. It can also lead to avoidance of triggers or situations that could cause emotional dysregulation and can result in further difficulties with emotional regulation.

Decreasing Emotional Vulnerability and Suffering

If you are feeling emotionally overwhelmed and vulnerable, you may be struggling to find any way to help ease your emotional pain. It may be enticing to turn to alcohol to numb the pain or to use food as a coping mechanism whenever you're stressed. Purchasing something new may also provide a temporary distraction. At first glance, these responses and coping mechanisms might seem innocent. However, if any of these become habitual, they could lead to more difficulties later on.

Fortunately, there are other strategies to cope with emotional hardship. That's exactly what we're going to discuss as we close out this chapter.

Find a New Hobby

A new hobby can be a great way to help deal with emotional pain and suffering. Hobbies are often activities that take up a lot of our time and provide us with a sense of purpose, satisfaction, and accomplishment. When we are feeling emotional pain, these activities provide us with a distraction from our thoughts and feelings. It gives us an outlet for our negative energy and allows us to focus our energy on something positive and creative. By introducing a new hobby, we are using our time in a mindful way that helps us to take better care of ourselves and process our emotions in a constructive way. Furthermore, hobbies can provide us with a sense of purpose and social connection. Whether it's finding a new hobby or revisiting a long-forgotten hobby, it can be a great way to connect with others who share the same interests. Having someone to share our experiences with and look forward to spending time with can be an important component of emotional healing.

Cry It Out

Crying it out can be a great way to help deal with emotional vulnerability. It allows you to get out whatever emotions you are feeling and express yourself in a safe and comfortable environment. When you cry, you are not only releasing pent-up tension but also releasing negative or toxic emotions. This helps to clear your mind and provide some clarity for how you want to handle the situation. It also gives you a sense of control and ownership over the emotion, as you are now in control of how you react to it. Crying it out is also beneficial because you remind yourself of the importance of self-care. You are taking the time to acknowledge the emotion and work through it, which helps to soften its impact. The act of crying can also be perceived as a form of self-acceptance, and it helps build self-compassion. Additionally, crying can help reduce stress levels because it can be emotionally and physically exhausting to repress feelings.

Help Your Community

Helping your community can help you cope with emotional suffering because it can be a great source of emotional fulfillment. Contributing to your community can give you a sense of accomplishment. It can also help you develop empathy as you consider the needs of other people who may be in need. As you spend time volunteering and interacting with people who are going through difficulties, you may come to appreciate your own life and the power of kindness in connecting with those who are suffering. Participating in helping your community also offers a degree of social support that can help you cope with emotional suffering. When you volunteer, you are surrounding yourself with like-minded people who offer understanding and compassion as you reach out and benefit others. This can help you to develop a more meaningful social network that can provide much-needed distraction, hope, and encouragement.

Create Something You Can Be Proud Of

Creating something that you can be proud of can help you deal with emotional pain in a number of ways. First, the process of creating something can provide an escape from the emotional pain that you may be feeling. When you allow yourself to focus your energy and attention on the creative task at hand, you can put your emotional distress on the back burner, which allows you to find a moment of peace amidst the chaos. Also, creating something can provide a tangible reminder of your worth and capabilities. By creating something concrete and unique, you prove to yourself that you are capable of amazing things and that you are much more than your emotional pain. This real, measurable proof of your worth can lead to an increased feeling of self-confidence and self-acceptance and help soothe the pain. It can come in the form of music, painting, or even a new business.

Declutter Your Physical Space

Decluttering your space can help you deal with emotional suffering by allowing you to create an environment of peace and tranquility. When clutter is present, it can be a source of distraction and stress that can increase feelings of anxiety and depression. By removing the clutter from your space, you can create an atmosphere of calm that can help soothe your emotions and make it easier to cope with life's challenges. Decluttering also has the added benefit of helping to reduce stress levels that can often be triggered by physical clutter, freeing up valuable mental energy. This can give your brain more space to focus on the positive elements of life, such as productive activities and healthy relationships. You can give yourself the psychological space to process your emotions in a more constructive manner. Decluttering can also provide a sense of accomplishment in having tangible proof of taking action to improve your space and give you a boost of confidence to tackle other areas of your life.

Chapter 8:

The Power of Self-Love

Self-love is a powerful and important tool that everyone should be aware of. It involves accepting yourself just as you are and treating yourself with kindness, compassion, and appreciation. It's about recognizing that you are valuable and worthy of being happy. Practicing self-love means that you are comfortable with who you are and confident enough to stand up for yourself and speak your truth.

When you love yourself, you make a conscious effort in taking care of yourself, listening to your inner voice, and tending to your needs. It could include spending time alone, indulging in activities you enjoy, or even saying no to something that doesn't feel quite right. You might set healthy boundaries and make decisions that you know will foster growth, respect, and appreciation for yourself.

Self-love isn't always easy, and it takes time to cultivate, but the long-term benefits are worth the effort. Once you start to practice self-love, you will begin to feel empowered and free. You will be more equipped to handle difficult situations with grace and confidence, and you will move away from self-doubt and indecision. Ultimately, self-love is a journey of self-awareness, self-discovery, and self-acceptance that will bring you great joy and contentment.

Self-love is a big part of maintaining good mental health. In order to be mentally healthy, you must learn to value and accept yourself for who you are. Moreover, developing self-love can help to combat negative thoughts. By being kind to yourself and accepting your flaws, you are equipped with the ability to combat negative thinking, which can become a destructive habit. By engaging in self-love, you can let go of fear, shame, and anxiety and instead focus on being kind to yourself.

In this chapter, we will delve deeper into the concept of self-love and its relation to your mental health. We will also discuss various self-love strategies that you can practice and implement in your everyday life. We will discuss what it means to silence your inner critic and how you can safely get outside of your comfort zone.

The Value of Self-Love in Mental Health

Self-love is loving yourself and accepting yourself for who you are. It means having a positive attitude toward yourself and taking care of yourself physically, emotionally, and spiritually. It's recognizing and honoring your needs, wants, and desires and treating yourself with kindness and respect. But most importantly, self-love is an effective way of honoring and taking care of your mental health.

One way that self-love encourages good mental health is that it contributes to the cultivation of self-compassion. Remember that self-love is a process of developing positive self-talk, speaking positively to yourself, and reframing negative thoughts into more helpful ones. This helps you to develop a sense of worth, increase confidence, and gain self-acceptance. As you learn to love yourself in a compassionate way, this allows you to be more compassionate to yourself when you make mistakes or experience challenges. Self-love is also about taking loving care of yourself and your needs. This includes permitting yourself to relax, enjoying doing activities that bring you pleasure, and engaging in self-care. When you prioritize the things you need and do the things that bring joy, you are strengthening your sense of self-worth and are more likely to respond to yourself in a compassionate way.

Self-love also has a way of allowing you to forgive yourself and to move on from mistakes more easily. When you practice self-love, it can help you to forgive yourself for past mistakes. It helps you to recognize that everyone makes mistakes and that you were simply acting out of human nature. Self-love encourages feelings of compassion and understanding toward yourself. You begin to recognize that mistakes are a part of life, and it is important to accept and learn from those experiences rather than condemn yourself. Moreover, self-love also helps to provide perspective and appreciate the positive aspects of your life. You recognize that your mistakes are not the only thing that defines you. It helps to remind you of your strengths and accomplishments, which will make it easier to forgive yourself and accept your mistakes.

Practicing self-love can also help you to embrace your personal boundaries better. It gives you the confidence and strength to stand up for yourself. When you practice self-love, you start to respect your own feelings and know that it's okay to put your needs first and prioritize them. That allows you to draw a clear line between what you are willing to accept and what you are not, giving you a clear idea of what your boundaries are. When you have a strong sense of self-love, you trust yourself and your decisions more and are more apt to follow through on withdrawing from situations that make you feel uncomfortable or violated. For instance, it allows you to be more assertive with people when communicating your boundaries because you know that valuing your own needs and wishes is an important part of protecting yourself. Also, self-love gives you the courage to set boundaries that you know are important. Instead of feeling the guilt and shame that can come from knowing certain people or situations are not good for you, you trust yourself enough to make the same call and stick to it, even when it's difficult.

Not a lot of people realize that you can also increase your emotional satisfaction by practicing self-love. Now, it's important to note that self-love is not selfishness, but rather a compassionate and accepting attitude toward yourself. When you find yourself feeling overwhelmed and out of control, self-love can be a helpful tool for creating an emotionally healthier and more balanced state of mind. One way that self-love can help with emotional regulation is by allowing you to recognize and accept your emotions without judgment. When you can observe and acknowledge your emotions, you can better understand them and respond to them more productively. Also, since self-love helps to build healthy boundaries, you are less likely to be put in positions where you feel like you are emotionally overwhelmed. On a deeper level, self-love emotionally supports you by encouraging you to connect with your own inner wisdom and intuition. This can lead to a greater sense of being in control of your own life and feeling more secure in your decisions.

Cultivating Self-Love: Strategies That Work

Now, as you may realize, self-love doesn't always come naturally to people. As weird as it may sound, a lot of people have genuine trouble with loving themselves. If this applies to you, then it's important that you consciously practice certain habits that enforce self-love in your life. In this section, we are going to go over some of the best practices when it comes to cultivating self-love in your own life.

Limit Your Self-Limiting Beliefs

You may not realize it, but your self-limiting beliefs can be a big barrier to your self-care goals. Start by acknowledging the self-limiting beliefs that are stopping you from achieving your self-care goals. Be honest with yourself and recognize the thoughts and feelings that come up when you think about achieving your goals. Once you have identified your limiting beliefs, take the time to challenge each one. Ask yourself "Is this really true?" and "Where did this belief come from?" Evaluate each belief critically and be open to the possibility that it may not be grounded in reality. After examining and challenging the limiting beliefs, start replacing them with new, positive ones. Develop affirmations and mantras that are supportive and compassionate. It'll be slow going at first replacing these beliefs, but with practice, you can begin to rewire your mindset and move closer to achieving your self-care goals. Don't forget to reward yourself for pushing through your self-limiting beliefs. Track your progress, celebrate small victories, and make sure to acknowledge your hard work. This will help to reinforce the new, positive beliefs and make it easier to keep up the momentum.

Practice Positive Self-Talk

You can practice positive self-talk by learning to speak kindly to yourself. Start by being mindful of your internal dialogue and being aware of when you have negative thoughts. Instead of just ignoring them or pushing them away, try replacing them with an alternate thought or affirmation that is more positive. Instead of saying "I'm so bad at this," try saying "I'm learning, and progress takes time."

You can also practice repeating positive affirmations to yourself. This can be done either out loud or to yourself in your head (or even written down). Make sure the affirmations are personal and meaningful to you and are phrased in the present tense. Examples of positive affirmations are "I am capable and deserving of happiness and success" or "I choose to focus on the good in my life today."

Create a Self-Love Music Playlist

Before you put together your self-love music playlist, it's important to take a few moments to identify the feelings and emotions you'd like to evoke. Self-love and self-care come in all shapes and sizes, making the process of finding the perfect music that reflects the feelings you're looking for a bit trickier. Make a list of words that reflect your current emotional state or the emotions you'd like to feel more of such as "peaceful," "energized," "loved," or "motivated."

Now that you have a list of emotions that resonate with you, it's time to find the perfect music for your self-love playlist. Start by looking for songs that reflect the emotions and feelings you'd like to experience. Be sure to include a variety of genres and styles so as not to make the playlist sound monotonous. Try to mix familiar songs with more obscure ones that you may never have listened to before.

Now you have a self-love playlist that is tailored to you! All that's left to do is enjoy it! Listen to your playlist in a quiet, comfortable space, and take some time to reflect and appreciate yourself. Allow yourself to feel the emotions your music invokes and be kind to yourself during the process.

Incorporate Meditation Into Your Routine

Starting a meditation routine is a great way to show yourself some self-love. To start incorporating it into your daily routine, make sure to set aside some dedicated time for yourself each day. Find a quiet, comfortable spot with minimal distractions and set the mood for meditation by creating a soothing atmosphere. To help settle your mind and start to focus on your breath, you can incorporate aromatherapy with essential oils, candles, or incense. Once you're in a relaxed state and your mind is clear, it's time to start your meditation practice. Sit in an upright and comfortable position, take a deep breath in, and release it slowly. Then begin your practice by focusing on your breath and allowing yourself to just be. You can also practice guided meditation by listening to a prerecorded audio or video to gain more mindful insight on the present moment. After meditating, take a few moments to be mindful of your surroundings and the sensations in your body. You'll be surprised at how much self-affirmation, self-awareness, and self-love can be achieved with just a few minutes a day dedicated to meditation.

Spend Time on Your Favorite Hobbies

Spending time on your favorite hobbies is also a form of self-love. It helps to nurture your body, mind, and soul and allows you to take a break from the everyday stresses of life. By engaging in activities that you enjoy doing, such as painting, crafting, playing a musical instrument, reading, or playing a game, you are giving yourself permission to relax and enjoy yourself. Participating in these activities is an important way to honor your needs and show yourself self-appreciation. It allows you to take a moment to focus on something that brings you joy, which in turn can help to reduce stress and allow you to be more productive in other areas of your life. Additionally, as you become more in tune with yourself, you may gain more insight into your strengths, weaknesses, and abilities. This can then help you to better recognize and appreciate your unique gifts and talents that make you who you are. Ultimately, taking the time to focus on your favorite hobbies is a wonderful way to show yourself a little love.

Take Yourself Out on a Date

Taking yourself out on a date is an incredibly powerful form of self-love. On a basic level, you are taking time out of a busy day or week to prioritize yourself and your needs. You show yourself the same care and attention that you would show someone you love. You'll have the opportunity to relax and reflect, explore something you're interested in, or just take some time to be alone. It's a chance to practice self-care, be kind to yourself, and give yourself some self-compassion. By bringing yourself out on a date, you're effectively demonstrating self-respect and building self-esteem—you're continuing to show yourself that you're important, worthy, and deserving of care and attention. Plus, taking yourself out on a date can help allow you to shift away from negative self-talk and into an appreciation for who you are. What's great about this form of self-love is that you don't need anyone else to get involved—the date is all about you, exactly as you are.

Make Self-Care a Priority

Self-care is essential for leading a healthy, balanced and happy life. So start by taking some time for yourself each day. Set aside at least 15 minutes for yourself to relax and refocus. Do something you enjoy, like reading, watching a movie, going for a walk, or journaling to take care of yourself and destress. Next, consider adopting a few healthy habits. Eating healthy meals, getting enough sleep, and exercising regularly can do wonders for your well-being. Even taking a few moments each day to meditate and practice mindfulness can have a positive impact. These aren't things that you should just do when you have extra time. You need to carve time out of your schedule to take care of yourself.

Conclusion

Mental health is one of the greatest challenges of our age, with millions of people around the world struggling daily with depression, anxiety, and other mental disorders. It is particularly prevalent among adults, where the pressures of work, family, and money can prove too much for some. This can result in an inability to cope and lead to physical and psychological problems, such as insomnia, substance abuse, and panic attacks. The severity of the problem can be seen in the number of people seeking help for mental health issues. One out of every five American adults is experiencing some kind of mental health issue (National Institute of Mental Health, 2022). The effects of mental health issues can be devastating, with a heightened risk of physical health problems, unemployment, homelessness, and even suicide. This risk is especially high among the elderly, who may struggle with depression, anxiety, and dementia.

In order to address this problem, there needs to be a greater focus on mental health awareness, education, and support. Governments should look to provide access to high-quality mental health services, as well as introduce initiatives to reduce the stigma attached to mental health issues. This can include more stringent regulations on insurance companies to make mental health care more affordable as well as training programs to help employers spot mental health issues in their workforce.

But more than just government assistance, there is also a need for greater public awareness and education so that people can recognize when they or a loved one may be experiencing mental health issues and feel comfortable seeking help. Ultimately, this will go a long way to creating a society that is more compassionate, understanding, and supportive of those suffering from mental health issues. That's the main motivation for writing this book. Hopefully, the contents of this book will have helped open your eyes to the serious issues surrounding mental health and how you aren't necessarily powerless against it.

It's important to remember that even during challenging times, there is hope for better days. You are not alone in your struggles, and there are many pathways to finding relief. There are people around you who understand and support you, and there are also a variety of resources available to help you. Having mental health problems is nothing to be ashamed of, and it is important that you take the time to recognize and understand your feelings. Reach out for help and take time for yourself to do activities that bring joy. Don't be afraid to ask for help; talking to a professional can be a great place to start. This book can certainly help as well. Your mental health is important. Be kind to yourself and know that healing is possible.

Mental health problems can be difficult and can sometimes feel like they will never end, but it is important to remember that there is always hope. Mental health issues are not permanent and can be managed with proper care and support. Everyone is able to heal, grow, and make progress in their recovery. Remember, no matter how tough the process may be, it is possible to tackle any mental health issues and come out the other side. With the right resources and understanding, you can get through this and make a full recovery. Hopefully, this book will have served as a valuable tool in helping you to get the help you or your loved ones need to get better. Don't be afraid to share this book and spread its positivity to those around you. We're all in this together.

References

American Psychological Association. (2022). *Schizophrenia.* American Psychological Association. https://www.apa.org/topics/schizophrenia#:~:text=Schizoph renia%20is%20a%20serious%20mental

Barrocas Gottlieb, A. L. (2018, January 17). *DBT 101: What is mindfulness?* Sheppard Pratt. https://www.sheppardpratt.org/news-views/story/dbt-101-what-is-mindfulness/#:~:text=In%20dialectical%20behavior%20thera py%20

BetterHelp Editorial Team. (2023, February 7). *What's the difference between primary and secondary emotions?.* BetterHelp. https://www.betterhelp.com/advice/general/what-are-primary-and-secondary-emotions/

Borchard, T. (2011, June 28). *Marsha Linehan: What is dialectical behavioral therapy (DBT)?* Psych Central. https://psychcentral.com/blog/marsha-linehan-what-is-dialectical-behavioral-therapy-dbt

Cuofano, G. (2023, April 3). *What is PERMA model? The PERMA model in A nutshell.* FourWeekMBA. https://fourweekmba.com/perma-model/

Emotional regulation skills. (2023). Dialectical Behavior Therapy (DBT) Tools. https://dbt.tools/emotional_regulation/index.php

Gibbon, P. (2020). *Martin Seligman and the rise of positive psychology. Humanities, 41*(3). National Endowment for the Humanities (NEH). https://www.neh.gov/article/martin-seligman-and-rise-positive-psychology

Heingartner, D. (2020, December 3). *IQ and EQ: New study finds that high-iq people also have more emotional intelligence.* Psych News Daily. https://www.psychnewsdaily.com/iq-and-eq-gifted-people-also-have-a-bit-more-emotional-intelligence/

Hobbs, C., Armitage, J., Hood, B., & Jelbert, S. (2022). A systematic review of the effect of university positive psychology courses on student psychological wellbeing. *Frontiers in Psychology, 13.* https://doi.org/10.3389/fpsyg.2022.1023140

Lopes, P. N., Brackett, M. A., Nezlek, J. B., Schütz, A., Sellin, I., & Salovey, P. (2004). Emotional Intelligence and Social Interaction. *Personality and Social Psychology Bulletin, 30*(8), 1018–1034. https://doi.org/10.1177/0146167204264762

Mead, E. (2020, January 11). *What is positive psychotherapy? (Benefits & model).* PositivePsychology.com. https://positivepsychology.com/positive-psychotherapy-research-effects-treatment/

Mindful Staff. (2020, July 8). *What is mindfulness?* Mindful. https://www.mindful.org/what-is-mindfulness/

National Institute of Mental Health. (2023, March). *Mental illness.* National Institute of Mental Health. https://www.nimh.nih.gov/health/statistics/mental-illness

Parvez, H. (2021, December 23). *Primary and secondary emotions (with examples).* PsychMechanics. https://www.psychmechanics.com/primary-and-secondary-emotions/

Raypole, C. (2020, April 28). *How to become the boss of your emotions.* Healthline. https://www.healthline.com/health/how-to-control-your-emotions

Russell, S. (2010, August 6). *4 tips to get in touch with your feelings instead of burying them.* Tiny Buddha. https://tinybuddha.com/blog/4-tips-to-get-in-touch-with-your-feelings-instead-of-burying-them/

Schenck, L. K. (2011, April 16). *Top 10 ways to regulate emotions—part one.* Mindfulness Muse. https://www.mindfulnessmuse.com/dialectical-behavior-therapy/top-10-ways-to-regulate-emotions-part-one

Spector, N. (2018, January 10). *Smiling can trick your brain into happiness—and boost your health.* Better by Today. https://www.nbcnews.com/better/health/smiling-can-trick-your-brain-happiness-boost-your-health-ncna822591

Sutton, J. (2016, September 26). *12 inspiring real-life positive psychology examples.* PositivePsychology.com. https://positivepsychology.com/positive-psychology-examples/

Thoreson, A. (2021, September 16). *Helping people, changing lives: 3 health benefits of volunteering.* Mayo Clinic Health System. https://www.mayoclinichealthsystem.org/hometown-health/speaking-of-health/3-health-benefits-of-volunteering#:~:text=Volunteering%20reduces%20stress%20and%20increases

Vaughn, S. (2022, November 30). *State Targets and goals of DBT: Creating a life worth living.* Psychotherapy Academy. https://psychotherapyacademy.org/dbt/targets-goals-of-dbt/

Zeidner, M., Roberts, R. D., & Matthews, G. (2008). The Science of Emotional Intelligence. *European Psychologist, 13*(1), 64–78. https://doi.org/10.1027/1016-9040.13.1.64